Curriculum Focus

Materials

Archie McIver

Curriculum Focus series

History

Toys Key Stage 1
Famous Events Key Stage 1
Famous People Key Stage 1
Invaders Key Stage 2
Tudors Key Stage 2

Geography

Islands and Seasides Key Stage 1
The Local Area Key Stage 1

Science

Ourselves Key Stage 1
Plants and Animals: Key Stage 1
Materials: Key Stage 1

Published by Hopscotch Educational Publishing Ltd,
Unit 2, The Old Brushworks, 56 Pickwick Road,
Corsham, Wilts SN13 9BX
Tel: 01249 701701

© 2004 Hopscotch Educational Publishing

Written by Archie McIver
Linked ICT activities by Michelle Singleton
Series design by Blade Communications
Illustrated by Susan Hutchison
Cover illustration by Susan Hutchison
Printed by Clintplan, Southam

Archie McIver hereby asserts his moral right to be identified as the author of this work in accordance with the Copyright, Designs and Patents Act, 1988.

ISBN 1-904307-38-8

All rights reserved. This book is sold subject to the condition that it shall not, by way of trade or otherwise, be lent, hired out or otherwise circulated without the publisher's prior consent in any form of binding or cover other than that in which it is published and without a similar condition, including this condition, being imposed upon the subsequent purchaser.

No part of this publication may be reproduced, stored in a retrieval system, or transmitted, in any form or by any means, electronic, mechanical, photocopying, recording or otherwise, without the prior permission of the publisher, except where photocopying for educational purposes within the school or other educational establishment that has purchased this book is expressly permitted in the text.

Contents

	Cross-curricular links	4
	Introduction	5
1	Sensing materials	7
2	The same but different	17
3	Magnetic materials	29
4	Material pick 'n' mix	41
5	Materials put to the test	53
6	Grouping materials	62
7	Material workout	71
8	Heating materials	81
9	Water world	92
10	All steamed up	100

Cross-curricular links

Chapter	Science SoW	Art SoW	Literacy framework	Numeracy framework	ICT SoW
1	Unit 1C		Y1, Term 1: T12, T14 Y1, Term 2: T22 Y1, Term 1: S4		Unit 1C
2	Unit 1C		Y1, Term 1: T12, T14 Y1, Term 2: T22		Unit 1D/2A
3	Unit 1C		Y1, Term 1: T12, T14 Y1, Term 2: T22 Y1, Term 1: S4		Unit 1F
4	Unit 1C		Y1, Term 1: S4		Unit 1B
5	Unit 1C		Y1, Term 1: T12, T14 Y1, Term 2: T22 Y1, Term 1: S4		Unit 2B
6	Unit 2D	Unit 1B	Y1, Term 1: S4 Y1, Term 1: T12, T14 Y1, Term 2: T22		Unit 2B
7	Unit 2D	Unit 1B	Y1, Term 1: S4 Y1, Term 1: T12, T14 Y1, Term 2: T22	Y1: Measures, shape and space	Unit 1C
8	Unit 2D		Y1, Term 1: T12, T14 Y1, Term 2: T22		Unit 1C
9	Unit 2D		Y1, Term 1: S4 Y1, Term 1: T12, T14 Y1, Term 2: T22		Unit 1E/2E
10	Unit 2D		Y1, Term 1: S4 Y1, Term 1: T12, T14 Y1, Term 2: T22		Unit 2B

Introduction

About this book

Curriculum Focus: Materials is about exploring the materials that make up our world. It enables teachers to lead their classes on an exciting journey of discovery. All the information, worksheets and lesson plans you need are provided, allowing you to focus on guiding the children. Although a wide variety of activities and experiments have been included, there is no requirement for the teacher to have scientific expertise or for the class to have access to scientific equipment.

This book is based on the QCA Schemes of Work. Chapters 1–5 are for Year 1 and cover Unit 1C: 'Sorting and Using Materials'. Chapters 6–10 are for Year 2 and cover unit 2D: 'Grouping and Changing Materials'. The work contained in this book ideally should come after work on Unit 1A: 'Ourselves' since the first chapter 'Sensing materials' depends on some familiarity with the five senses. Apart from that, the children are not presumed to have any other scientific background.

The chapters are designed to develop scientific skills in achievable steps. The skills include ways of recording results, concepts such as fairness and, in later chapters, the children are encouraged to sum up the key ideas in a conclusion. More able pupils can improve and extend their investigations using the guidance provided. Using the activities in *Curriculum Focus: Materials* will help to develop the skills the children will need; these skills are just as important as the concepts and knowledge they acquire. All will be used in their later scientific studies.

In the book you will find everything you need to run successful science lessons, from clear background information and full descriptions to differentiated activity sheets. Importantly, the hands-on work has been tested to ensure that it works effectively. The children will need some objects and sample materials to examine and test but care has been taken to limit these to ones readily available in the school environment or, occasionally, items such as chocolate or a cake mix, that can easily be acquired from a supermarket.

Each chapter of the book contains:

- detailed teachers' notes containing the background you need to explain the concepts you are covering;

- comprehensive lesson plans with descriptions that include how to introduce a lesson, how to resource and run the activities, how to sum up the key ideas, ways of extending the lesson and links with ICT;

- activity sheets based on the same core work, but differentiated to accommodate children attaining at three different levels (Activity sheet 1 for lower-attaining children, Activity sheet 2 for most children and Activity sheet 3 for higher-attaining children);

- a variety of generic sheets where an opportunity has been found to support the learning process.

Understanding materials

Science is about understanding what is around us; there is no better place to start than with the materials that make up our world. Babies and toddlers spend much of their time investigating materials: touching and tasting, splashing and pouring, twisting and bashing, knocking things down and building things up. The world is a treasure trove of materials and they explore it endlessly and with great enthusiasm. Children know a lot about materials as a result of these early 'tests' but most of this learning occurs before they have the language to describe it. As a result, their ability to express themselves often falls well below what they actually know.

Having this prior knowledge of materials has its benefits: children often recognise material types, such as stone, wood, glass and water, with little difficulty. It does, however, have its limitations: children have rarely considered how they know that stone is stone; they 'just know' that it is. The earliest part of this book challenges children to use different senses and descriptive words to describe materials.

This takes the form of games that are great fun, but are important because they home in on not just the language, but also on the understanding of 'how we know'.

Grouping materials follows and makes use of these abilities to recognise and classify materials according to 'what they are like', or their 'properties'. The book moves from observation to simple experiments where materials are tested prior to putting them into groups (for example, magnetic and non-magnetic).

The last chapters in the book look at how humans change materials by heating and cooling and, in particular, how heat is involved in the changes between solids, liquids and gases.

Each chapter has been carefully designed to build understanding, vocabulary and skills. As a result, it is best to progress through the chapters in the order they have been presented.

Science is exciting

Science is exciting, especially when it takes you into the unknown. Excitement and predictability are not usually mutual experiences. Science is exciting partly because of that unpredictability. It can be thought of as an unfolding story, a mystery, a revelation, and it is the twists in the plot, the unexpected and the unknown that give it its zest. Science only advances when it moves into the unknown.

This book sets activities and experiments for all the class, but encourages these to be used as a platform for the children's own ideas. Children have tremendous imagination and are always keen to explore and to try out 'just to see what happens'. The book gives them a wide range of investigations but, wherever possible, you are encouraged to let them go a little further (for example, try other materials, do extra tests, allow different conditions).

When testing to see which materials were waterproof (Chapter 5 'Materials put to the test') some surprise results turned up (some fluffy materials were remarkably waterproof; some shiny ones were not). The children were intrigued and came up with suggestions for extending the test to include dripping water from a height-making the test conditions more like real rain. They were thinking creatively as well as scientifically. It was exciting, it was discovery, it was the stuff of real science.

You too can use *Curriculum Focus: Materials* as an enjoyable way of learning and as a platform to explore and to fire the imagination of your children.

Sensing materials

TEACHERS' NOTES

What are materials?

Materials are the substances from which things are made, including solids, liquids, gases and combinations of these (such as in a car). The study of materials overlaps with many other fields – for example, living things are made from materials and therefore biologists study the complex materials of which living organisms are made. The study of materials could cover a vast range of substances, but more often concentrates on the materials that humans find useful.

At Key Stage 1 we deal mostly with solid materials, but towards the end of the Key Stage (and this book) there is some work on materials changing between the solid and liquid states.

What does the word 'material' mean?

The scientific meaning of 'material' is 'the matter from which things are made'. Unfortunately, the word 'material' has several other meanings that may cause confusion. Non-scientific meanings of the word 'material' include:

- fabric, clothing, textiles (a much narrower meaning of the word);
- information sources (as in 'reference materials');
- tools/equipment (as in 'photographic materials', 'writing materials').

The distraction of shape

If you hold up a plastic cup to the class and ask what it is, the children will quite correctly reply 'a cup', although it could also be described correctly as 'a piece of plastic'. It is natural for children to identify items by their shape and function – the material they are made from is almost always a secondary consideration. Since this topic is about the material, it would be useful to start with chunks (cubes, pieces, and so on) of the material rather than objects, so that the shape is not too much of a distraction. Children tend not only to see the object first, but when asked about the material they may well use their knowledge about the object and a process of deduction to 'identify' the material. If asked about a saucepan, they will often guess that it is made from metal because they already know that most saucepans are made from metal. If, however, they are given a square of the same material, they have to examine the material more closely and use clues about the material itself to identify it.

Identifying materials

To identify materials we must use our senses, though not all of them are very useful/practical:

- sight – probably the most important sense, for seeing colour and texture;
- touch – important for telling the surface texture, the flexibility, the density and how well it conducts heat (see the definition of thermal conductivity on Generic sheet 2);
- taste – some materials have a distinctive taste but it would probably be unwise to use this from a health and hygiene viewpoint;
- smell – some materials have a smell (such as leather, plastic, wool) but in humans this sense isn't strong or reliably used;
- hearing – materials don't give off sound of their own accord but some have a distinctive sound when tapped (such as the ringing sound of metal).

Naming basic materials

Some material groups are fairly straightforward.

- Metals – a widely used term covering a large group with features that are fairly easy to recognise, the most obvious being the shiny 'metallic' surface (all clean metals have this). They are also dense, good conductors of heat and electricity, and tend to be tough and flexible. It is not necessary to identify the individual types of metal though some children will happily use specific names such as steel, iron, gold and silver.

- Glass – a well-known group and usually easy to identify. There are different types of glass (heat-resistant Pyrex, toughened glass, fibreglass) but most common types look the same and have similar properties of hardness, transparency and brittleness.

- Plastic – a widely used term for materials that are usually easy enough to recognise. A key issue is that they cover such a wide range of forms, colours and types that it may be difficult to see why they all come under the same name (see 'Naming complex materials' below). Children may be familiar with some specific names such as polythene, nylon, PVC and polystyrene, but at this level it is sufficient to use the term 'plastic'.

- Sand – a well-known term and easily identified.

- Wood – a common term, and types are relatively easy to identify by their colour, feel and pattern (see 'Naming complex materials' below).

- Paper – a common term and easily identified.

- Rubber – its highly elastic properties are familiar, used to make the soles of shoes and tyres.

- Fabric – woven fibres to make clothing and upholstery; can be made from many materials so not strictly speaking one group but at this level it is probably best to keep it as one.

Some material groups are more problematic.

- Rock or stone – many different colours and textures exist. A common building material in the past. The words may be more familiar to children as objects ('a rock' and 'a stone' for pebbles and boulders) than as a material. There can also be confusion with similar manufactured materials, such as concrete and brick.

- Concrete – grey, uniform and easily confused with rock, stone or brick. Can be mixed and poured into a mould to set, providing pre-cast beams for large constructions such as bridges, or building blocks (about twice the size of a house brick, with a grey, lumpy finish).

- Brick – its shape, size and colour are special features. Made from baked clay. Can be confused with rock, stone and concrete, especially if only a fragment is provided.

- Clay – a natural soft material which can be shaped and then set hard by baking at high temperatures. Commonly used to make crockery and kitchenware, but although easy to recognise there is no ideal term that encompasses the whole group. 'Clay' is perhaps the best term, though the word is more correctly used for the material in its soft, pre-fired form. 'Ceramics' is a more accurate term as it covers fired clay but is not so commonly used and is perhaps a bit technical at this level. Specific types of clay have fairly popular names but are difficult for the non-expert to differentiate – earthenware, china, stoneware and porcelain. The term 'pottery' further complicates things as the term comes from the word 'pots' and is typically applied to handcrafted ceramics.

Naming complex materials

Our ability to develop a huge range of new materials has made the task of identifying material types more complex. Composites have become increasingly common (materials that are a mix of different materials). It is probably best to avoid providing these as samples in class exercises, except possibly for the more able. Children may ask about them as they are becoming increasingly common. It is usually possible to put these composite materials into one of the main groups according to the main material used in their production. For example:

- Composite wood products (chipboard, blockboard, fibreboard, MDF). These usually look and feel enough like wood to be identified easily. Most are made by chopping or pulping wood and then gluing it in sheets. Often used as sheeting for building. Should be classed as wood.

- Laminated wood products. These are usually composite wood products (see above) coated with plastic such as Formica. Very commonly used for kitchen worksurfaces, doors, tables, shelving, flat-pack furniture. Should be classed as wood or wood/plastic.

- Coated materials. Many materials that children encounter will have coatings, making them less easy to identify. Metals are very commonly painted or given other coatings for the sake of appearance or to protect them from rusting (radiators, white goods in the kitchen, cars, bikes). Wood is often painted or varnished. Packaging may be cardboard but with plastic or metal foil coatings (fruit juice cartons). Glass bottles are sometimes shrink-wrapped with plastic.

- Materials that mimic. Manufacturers often produce less expensive materials that are designed to look like the real thing. Plastic-coated wood often has a grain pattern and colour to mimic solid wood. Bathroom fittings (taps), toys and watches are sometimes made from plastic with a metallic coating and can look very like solid metal.

Sensing materials

> **Science objectives (Unit 1C)**
> - To know that every material has many properties, which can be recognised using our senses and described using appropriate vocabulary.
> - To record observations of materials.
> - To ask questions and to explore materials and objects using appropriate senses, making observations and communicating these.
> - To know that there are many materials and that these can be named and described.

Resources

- Sample materials (pieces of materials rather than identifiable objects) – about six per group
- A selection of about ten objects made from different materials
- Generic sheets 1–3 (pages 11–13)
- Activity sheets 1–3 (pages 14–16)
- Cardboard boxes to make window boxes, one per group, with an opening in the top and a hole about 3cm x 3cm cut in one side
- Labels written on card (metal, plastic, wood, paper, glass, clay, rock, fabric, sand)
- Ideally, the objects illustrated on the activity sheets.

Starting points: *whole class*

Use a selection of five to ten objects to introduce the idea of what we mean by 'materials'. Have some simple examples, such as wooden, plastic and metal spoons, and some slightly more challenging examples, such as a painted metal toy car or a metal spoon with a plastic/wooden handle. Show the objects to the class and discuss what they are and what they are made from, drawing their attention to the words we use to describe them.

The emphasis here is on information from the senses. It would be a good idea to go over the five senses and discuss which are most appropriate here.

Ask questions such as:

- What is the object called?
- What is it made from?
- How can you tell what it is made from?
- What senses are you using?
- What colour is it?

Now move on to identify materials without having clues from the shape of the object. Use material samples if available (squares or shapes that are not specific objects). Samples are preferable since children can handle and examine the materials. However, if a suitable range is not available, use the window box method. This can be used to show the class samples of a material without them seeing the object. Put items inside the box, taking care not to let the children see the object until the material has been identified. Let them put their fingers through the hole in the side to touch the item. They may want to guess what the object is but emphasise that this is not the aim.

Sum up by discussing which senses are most useful for identifying a material and the words that describe what each sense detects – for example, the sense of touch can tell us if it is rough or smooth, warm or cold.

Group activities

Activity sheet 1
This activity is aimed at children who can recognise the simpler material types (wood, plastic, stone, metal, glass) and can use descriptive words from a list to guess basic material types. Ideally, have examples of each object on the sheet for the children to examine.

Activity sheet 2
This activity is aimed at children who can recognise most of the common material types (wood, plastic, stone, metal, glass) and can, with support, correctly record their properties using a good range of vocabulary. Ideally, have examples of each object on the sheet for the children to examine.

Activity sheet 3
This activity is aimed at children who can recognise most of the common material types and a number of less obvious materials and can correctly describe a wide range of these materials' properties using appropriate vocabulary. Ideally, have examples of each object on the sheet for the children to examine.

Plenary session

Mystery material game
At this stage of the whole-class work, the emphasis is on the words we use to describe materials.

Using a box with just an opening in the top, ask a volunteer to be the 'sensor' for the class. Explain that the sensor's job is to use their senses to answer questions from the class about the material, but the sensor must not tell the class directly what the material is. The sensor can look down into the box and is allowed to see, feel and handle the object but should take care not to allow the class to see it. Acceptable questions are 'Is it soft?' and 'Is it clear?' Unacceptable questions include 'What is it like?' and 'What do you use it for?'

Give the rest of the class copies of Generic sheet 3. Invite them to ask sensor-specific questions using descriptive words (see Generic sheet 1, and Generic sheet 2 for more able children). The sensor should try to answer the questions with brief, factual answers, preferably using yes, no or one-word answers. As each question is answered, the descriptive words should be written up (for example, on a whiteboard) thus building up a descriptive profile of the material. When enough descriptive words have been obtained, the children should be able to guess the material's identity and then the name of the material should be added above the list of descriptive words on the display.

Some children may be tempted to guess the material before they have sufficient information to do so reliably. Don't allow guesses until at least three questions have been answered.

Gather a few of the materials used in the game and go over some of the descriptive words. Point out that everything around us is made from materials and ask the children to point out a material in use in the classroom. Then ask for words to describe the material's properties.

Ideas for support

If the children have difficulty recognising the name of the material then this could be written on the bottom of the object so that they can look if they are stuck. Copies of Generic sheet 1 should help them to devise questions and record descriptive words. A display could be made up of a few sample objects and labels added to give the name of the material and terms describing the properties of the material.

Ideas for extension

Challenge these children to do a class survey on what materials are in their pencil cases (or choose another source/area), recording and displaying the number of occurrences of each.

They could take a complex object, such as a metal toy car, draw a diagram of it and label all the materials used to make it.

They could investigate historical, unusual or specially developed materials using an encyclopedia, CD-Rom encyclopedia or the internet. Terms to look up are: gold, silver, lead, tungsten, alloy, Teflon, tungsten carbide, diamond, graphite, fibreglass and carbon fibre.

Linked ICT activities

Provide the children with about ten objects made from different materials. Organise them into five or six groups and give each group a different object, taking care not to let each see what the others have been given. Using a tape recorder ask the children to describe their object using some of the descriptive words they have been introduced to during this chapter. Encourage them to describe the material, explaining how the object feels and so on. When all the recordings have been completed, put the objects onto a table and play them back. Can the class guess which of the objects on the table the children in the different groups are describing?

Sensing materials

Here are some basic words for describing materials.

WORD BANK	
hard	soft
rough	smooth
shiny	dull
bendy	stiff
stretchy	not stretchy
strong	weak
thin	thick
coloured	colourless
clear	not clear
cold to the touch	warm to the touch
heavy	light
metallic	non-metallic

Sensing materials

Here are some more words for describing materials.

brittle – brittle materials shatter when hit or bent – for example, glass. WARNING: do not try to test for brittleness. This test would need adult help and safety measures such as goggles.

conducts electricity (electrical conductor) – allows electricity to flow through it easily. Metals are good conductors of electricity. Plastics, wood and paper are poor conductors of electricity. WARNING: never play with electricity.

conducts heat (thermal conductor) – allows heat to flow through it easily. Metals are good conductors of heat and feel cold to the touch (they take the heat away from your body). Plastics, wood and paper are poor conductors of heat and feel warm to the touch.

dense – materials that are dense feel heavy for their size. Metal is denser than plastic so a metal toy will feel much heavier than a plastic toy of the same size.

elastic – can be stretched or bent but returns to the same length or shape afterwards.

fibrous – made of fibres (thin strands of material).

flexible – a material that can bend easily.

malleable – material that can be squeezed into another shape – for example, clay. Metals are malleable though it takes large forces to shape them.

opaque – does not let light shine through it.

tough – materials that do not snap, crack or break easily.

translucent – lets light shine through but doesn't have to be clear – for example, a frosted glass window is translucent but not clear.

Sensing materials

3 GENERIC SHEET

Play the mystery material game!

The rules:
- One person is allowed to touch or see the material.
- The rest of the group should ask questions about the material and try to guess what it is. They should write their answers in the table.
Use the words on Generic sheet 1 to help you think of questions.

	Name of material			
Words to describe material				

PHOTOCOPIABLE

CURRICULUM FOCUS • MATERIALS 13

Name _____

Sensing materials

ACTIVITY SHEET 1

Match each picture to the material from which it is made.
There is one picture for each material.

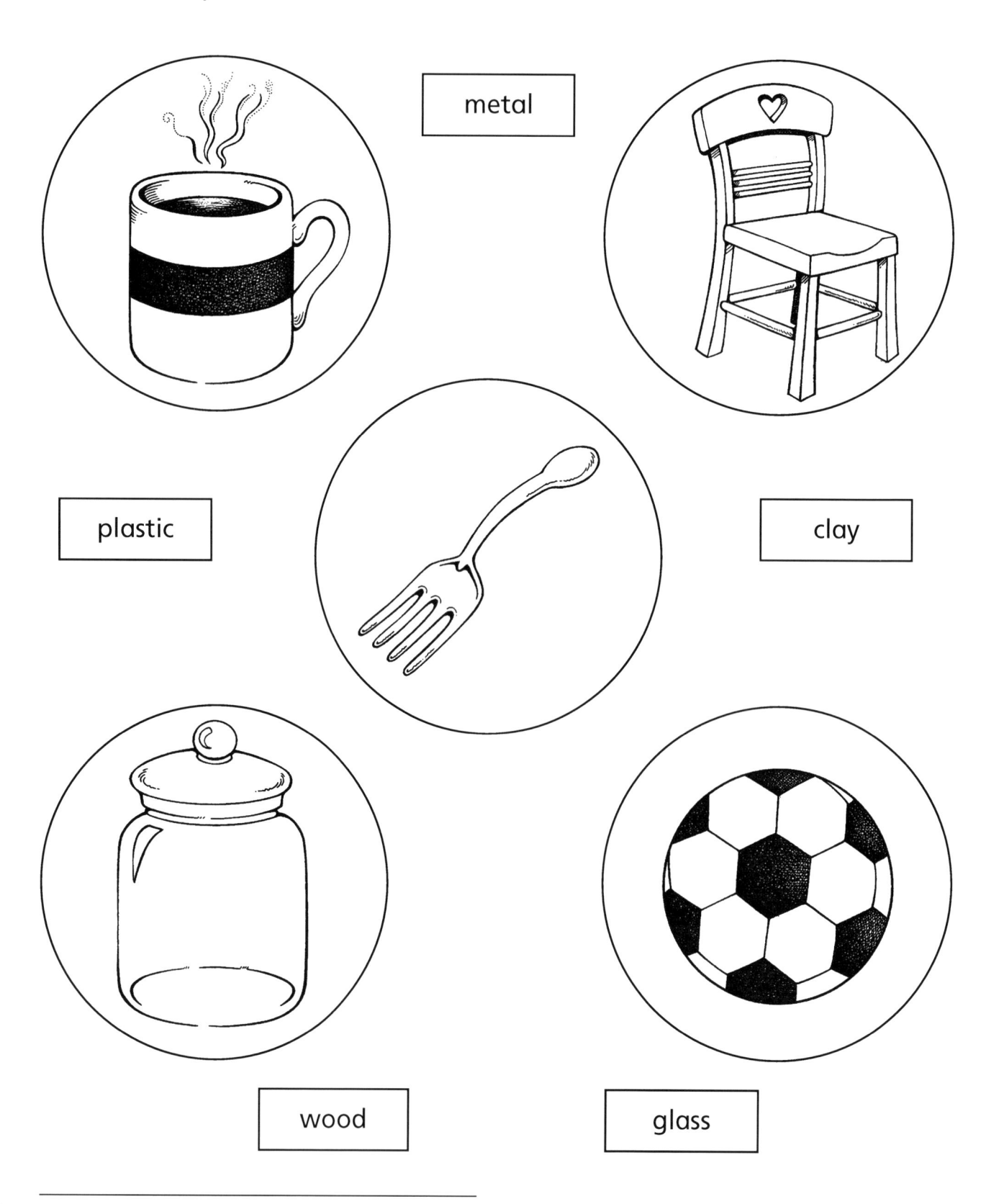

metal

plastic

clay

wood

glass

14 CURRICULUM FOCUS • MATERIALS

PHOTOCOPIABLE

Name _____

Sensing materials

Draw a line to connect each object to the material from which it is made. Draw a line to connect each object to a describing word. One of the objects is made from two different materials. Draw two lines to show both.

| wood | metal | plastic | glass | clay |

| shiny | clear | stretchy | dull | brittle |

PHOTOCOPIABLE

CURRICULUM FOCUS • MATERIALS 15

Name _____

Sensing materials

3 ACTIVITY SHEET

On another sheet of paper, write a sentence about each object shown below. Include the object's name, the material from which it is made, and something about that material. Remember that some of the objects are made from two different materials.

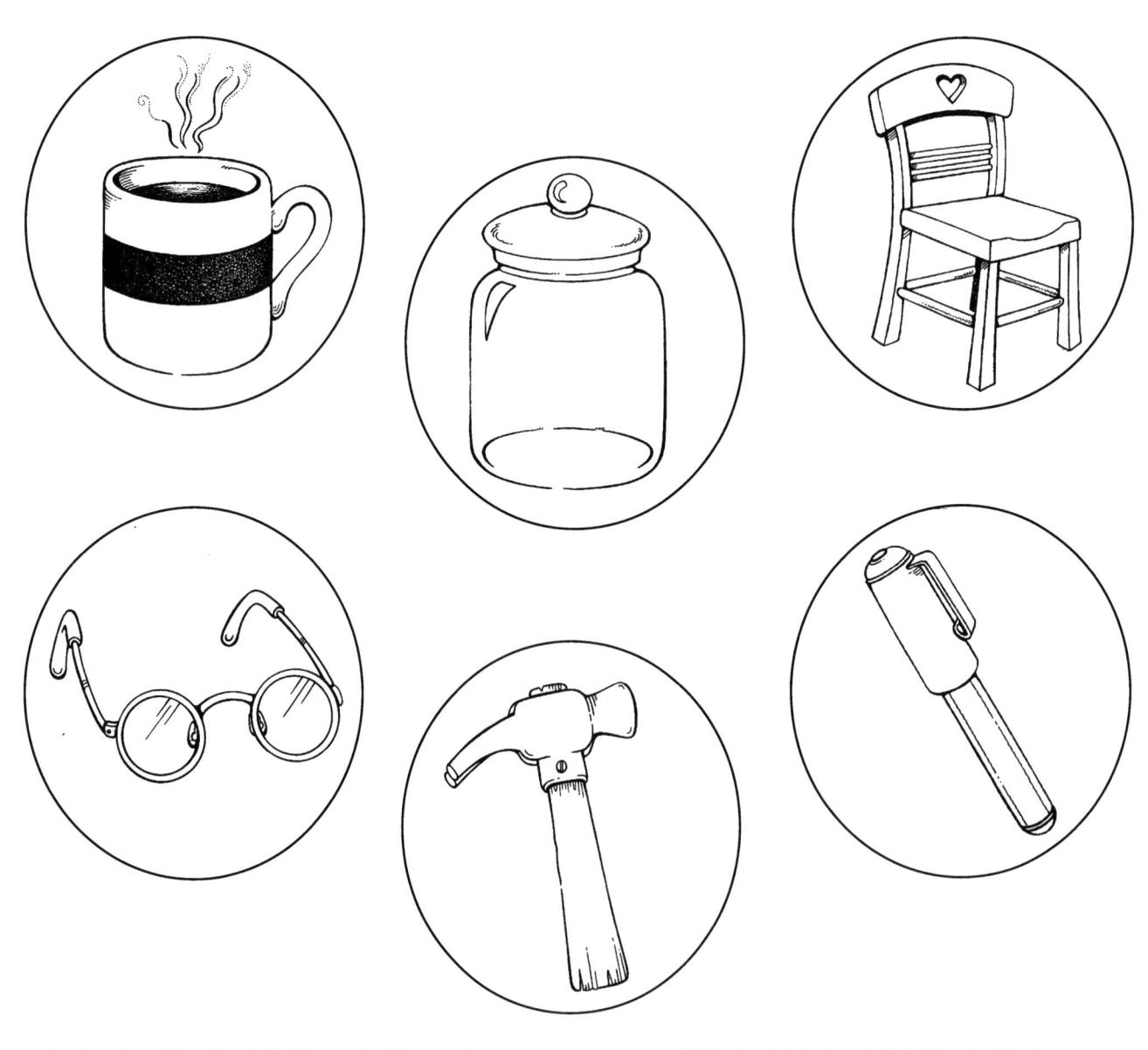

MATERIALS	
wood	metal
glass	plastic
clay	

PROPERTIES	
shiny	bendy
dull	heavy
smooth	metallic

16 CURRICULUM FOCUS • MATERIALS

PHOTOCOPIABLE

The same but different

TEACHERS' NOTES

Materials can be used in different ways and grouped using many different criteria. Chapter 1 will have given children some exposure to the idea of putting things into groups – by calling materials metal, plastic and so on, they are effectively defining groups. In this chapter we ask them to create groups in three ways – by material type (such as metal, wood, paper), by function (such as cups made from various materials) and by material properties (such as shiny materials and dull materials).

Grouping materials

Materials can be grouped in many different ways. Perhaps the most basic scientific grouping is by their state – solid, liquid or gas. Since liquids and gases aren't dealt with at this stage, this grouping system would be inappropriate. Other ways of grouping are by their source (such as natural materials and manufactured materials – see Chapter 6), by their chemical behaviour or structure (but not until Key Stages 3 and 4) and by the type of processing they have undergone, such as materials woven into fabrics. For now, it would be best to group materials by their properties. Objects are generally made with a particular task in mind, so the objects made from the materials can be grouped by their function.

Grouping materials by identifying characteristics (properties)

Finding the properties of a material is normally pretty straightforward since our senses usually tell us all we need to know. The tricky part is putting these properties into groups. Unfortunately, like real life, the properties of materials are not always black and white – it is those grey areas that can cause problems. Gradual variation in properties is common. If 'shiny' or 'dull' are the group headings, then a 'satin' or 'semi-matt' material such as polythene doesn't fit too clearly into either group. Avoid such examples initially, but it is probably better to introduce a few at some point and allow for discussion time and support.

Grouping materials by function (what the object is used for)

This is probably the easiest way to group items and can be used to demonstrate how a range of different materials can be suitable for the same task, such as a paper cup, plastic cup, metal cup and clay (porcelain) cup. Of course, here we depend on the shape of the object to give us the clue as to what its function is.

Vocabulary

Group

The word 'group' is widely used in everyday life and generally has a meaning similar to that used in this topic. It is an unusual word in that we use the same word for the verb 'to group' as we do for the noun 'a group'. The term 'group' as used in this unit means 'to classify', that is the process of collecting items together according to certain common traits (the verb) or a collection of items with common traits (the noun).

Other meanings of the word 'group' are:

- any collection of things, not necessarily having anything in common except location;
- pop group;
- pupil group within the class.

Comparative terms

In Chapter 1 special words were used to describe materials. Encourage the children to extend this to comparative terms so that from 'hard' the children extend their vocabulary by using 'harder' and 'hardest' (see Generic sheet 1).

Making groups

Making groups is a useful and natural thing to do. It is also more than just a matter of being tidy or organised because it makes us examine things more closely and think more analytically. Making groups leads to greater understanding.

Selecting group headings is a skill in itself and it is quite likely that children left to decide on their own headings with a random selection of objects will run into difficulties.

Simple grouping

There are two easier grouping exercises – grouping by:

- the type of material
- the function of the objects.

These are recommended for early work (see pages 7 and 8 for background on material types).

More advanced grouping

Grouping by identifying characteristics is a more difficult grouping exercise but is suggested in the Schemes of Work. Because difficulties can arise, guidelines have been provided in the grouping techniques section below.

Grouping techniques

Children may assume that, given a selection of objects, there is one correct way of putting them into groups. In real life there are usually a large number of acceptable ways to group a set of objects.

Opposite groups

When using the properties of the materials to create groups it is safer to go for just two groups and, where possible, to choose characteristics that are opposites, such as hard/soft or shiny/dull. It is feasible and sometimes even desirable to go for more than two groups, such as with colour where, for example, red/yellow/green/blue groups might be used.

Exclusive grouping technique

The name of this technique does not need to be mentioned to the children but the method is simple and is recommended because it is an effective technique for creating group headings (see Generic sheet 2). It also helps to avoid some of the most common problems (see overlapping groups and groups that aren't wide enough, below).

Exclusive grouping can also be more effective than using opposites like 'rough' and 'smooth' as described above although it looks very similar. The technique is to define a group and then to define the other group as everything else, such as 'smooth' and 'not smooth'. One advantage is that it can cope more easily with intermediate properties, such as a piece of wood that is just a little bit rough and therefore will not fit well into either 'rough' or 'smooth' groups – unless it is perfectly smooth it can still be classed as 'not smooth'. See below for other advantages.

Overlapping groups

Discourage children from creating groups that overlap because it means items could end up being in more than one group. For example, if the group headings were 'dull things' and 'thin things', wood could go into the dull group, but paper could fit into both groups. Even where children do not have a sample that causes an immediate overlap problem, it is still better to encourage the use of groups that don't overlap. The exclusive grouping technique described above prevents overlap.

Groups that aren't wide enough

Problems frequently occur when children are given a random selection of items and are sent off to put them into groups. They often identify two or three obvious groups into which they can put some items but are then left with the odds and ends that don't seem to have much in common. They may be tempted to create separate group headings for each of the remaining items or give up – neither outcome is desirable. Of course, this problem can easily be avoided by using the exclusive groups technique described above. Alternatively, problems can be avoided by carefully selecting the sample items and giving suitable guidance on the choice of groupings.

Decisions, decisions

There is no getting away from the fact that making groups involves making decisions – something that young children can find difficult, spend a lot of time on and argue over. It is less of a problem with grouping by function or material since it is often clear enough that a cup is a cup and that a piece of wood is indeed a piece of wood. But when it comes to properties – just how hard is hard? At a more advanced level, scientists move away from this simple 'one thing or its opposite' classification. They acknowledge that there is a gradual range of properties, and take measurements to see where the material comes in that range. For example, there is a ten-point scale of hardness called the Mohs scale. This overcomes the decision-making problem to some extent, because it no longer depends on personal judgement (see Chapter 5, where an attempt is made to measure the properties of a material). For now, be prepared to act as a referee if decision making becomes contentious!

The same but different

LESSON PLAN

> **Science objectives (Unit 1C)**
> - To know that objects are made from materials, and that different, everyday objects can be made from the same materials.
> - To know that materials can be used in a variety of ways.
> - To group materials together and make a record of groupings.
> - To know that materials can be sorted in a variety of ways according to their properties.
> - To use appropriate vocabulary to describe materials.

Resources

- Examples of the same object made from different materials (at least three different types of each object) such as cups made from plastic, glass, paper and ceramic, and balls made from rubber, plastic and leather
- Examples of the same materials being used for different objects (at least three different objects made from each material) such as a plastic toy, spoon, bag and cassette, and a metal key, bolt and spoon
- A selection of objects for group activities. These should be made from a variety of materials (about ten items per group covering three or four material types)
- Generic sheets 1–4 (pages 22–25)
- Activity sheets 1–3 (pages 26–28)
- Scissors and glue
- Pairs of written labels (dull/not dull, hard/not hard, bendy/not bendy, soft/not soft, shiny/not shiny, rough/not rough, stretchy/not stretchy, strong/not strong, weak/not weak, thin/not thin, thick/not thick, clear/not clear, cold/not cold, warm/not warm, heavy/not heavy)
- Ideally, all the items on Generic sheet 4

Starting points: *whole class*

Tell the class that they will be putting materials into groups. Show them a random selection of objects, such as a ball, ruler, key, bottle, toy car, plate, glove, ring, jar, coins, nail, marble and mug. Ask them to think about how the objects might be put into groups. This is just to set the ball rolling; it is not necessary to sort all of the objects into groups. It is sufficient to recognise that some items could belong to the same group as others and to state what they have in common. Stress that there are many ways of putting items into groups. Also encourage and support the children's confidence – some of them may be under the impression that their own idea is wrong because it is different from another correct answer.

Next show them a collection in which the same object is made from different materials (such as cups made from plastic, glass, paper and ceramic). You can tell them that this is a special selection you made earlier.

Ask questions such as:

- Do you think these are a group?
- Are these all the same?
- What is the same about them?
- What is different about them?
- Can you think of any other things that could be part of this group?

Show the class a second collection, but this time one where the same material has been used to make different objects (such as a set consisting of a plastic toy, spoon, bag and cassette or a set consisting of a metal key, bolt and spoon).

Ask the questions again and discuss how this second way of grouping objects compares with the first way. At this stage, you may decide to reinforce these ideas using Generic sheet 3 or additional collections of objects.

Now tell the class you are going to show them a third way of grouping. This is a simple way of dividing a group of things into two groups. Divide around eight objects of different materials into, for example, 'wood' and 'not wood' or 'bendy' and 'not bendy'. Draw attention to this 'X/not X' idea of grouping and recommend it as a good method. Use Generic sheet 2 to reinforce the method. They may explore other grouping systems but they might run into difficulties (see teachers' notes).

Before moving on to the group activities remind the children that they have been grouping things in three different ways:

- by what they are used for (the cups are all used for drinking)
- by what they are made from (the second collection was all plastic or metal objects)
- by what they are like – for example, shiny and not shiny materials.

Group activities

Activity sheet 1
This activity is aimed at children who can identify simple and obvious material types and their usage. They should cut out and stick in the pictures from Generic sheet 4 of items that could be made of plastic. Allow for flexibility of choice since many objects that might in the past have been made from other materials are now made from plastic. They should colour in the pictures choosing two colours – one for bendy objects and one for not bendy objects. They then use the word bank to record different materials that could be used to make cups. Ideally, have examples of each object from Generic sheet 4 for the children to examine.

Activity sheet 2
This activity is aimed at children who can identify most basic material types and have some understanding of the fact that materials can be grouped by type, function and properties. It is the concepts that are important, not the terminology, so they can call it grouping by 'what they are used for' rather than 'function', and 'what they are like' instead of 'properties'.

They should write or stick in pictures (from Generic sheet 4) in two groups – plastic and metal. They should write four materials that cups can be made from (without the help of pictures). They should group about ten objects into 'shiny' and 'not shiny'.

Activity sheet 3
This activity is aimed at children who can identify a good range of material types and who are capable of making decisions about grouping and recording results. They should have a good understanding of the fact that materials can be grouped by type, function and properties. Although it is the concepts that are important rather than the terminology, children could be encouraged to expand their vocabulary to include 'function' or 'usage' and 'properties' or 'characteristics'. They should also use comparative vocabulary (see Generic sheet 1).

They should group ten or more objects into 'shiny' and 'not shiny'. Then on the back of the sheet they should group other objects into 'hard' and 'not hard'; 'bendy' and 'not bendy'; 'rough' and 'not rough'. They should write down materials that spoons can be made from (some spoons have more than one material). On the back of the sheet they should list all the plastic objects that might be found in a kitchen.

Plenary session

Do the mystery material game as described on page 10 in the following way.

With the box have the following objects: plastic cup, porcelain cup, paper cup, paper-clip, envelope (paper), plastic wallet, plastic spoon and metal spoon. Put one item at a time into the box (unseen) and challenge the children to identify it. After a minimum of three questions allow some guesses. As each material is identified put it by its label.

Repeat the exercise for the same items but this time allowing questions about the shape and the material. The challenge is to identify what the item is used for, not what it is made from. As each item is identified it should be put beside a label describing its use:
- for drinking
- for holding paper
- for stirring.

Ideas for support

Put lists of the material types and the words used to describe them in prominent positions in the class.

Use Generic sheets 2 and 3 as examples of how things can be grouped.

Provide labelled materials for children who are unsure of identifying or spelling.

Display a list of material names and samples for reference.

Provide lists of words to describe materials (see the generic sheets from Chapter 1 and Generic sheet 1 from this chapter).

Provide sample displays of the three methods of grouping materials:

- different objects that are made from the same material
- one type of object being made from a variety of materials
- materials that have been grouped according to their properties.

Ideas for extension

These children could create posters using pictures to demonstrate the grouping systems. Shopping catalogues are one possible source of information and images.

Play the 'odd one out' game. Set up groups of materials/objects in which one item doesn't fit the group. The challenge is for the children to identify the odd one out and to explain why it doesn't fit.

They could investigate other examples of things being grouped – for example, supermarket products, or items in catalogues. Are they grouped by material type, function, properties or another criterion?

Linked ICT activities

Using word processing software, such as 'Talking Write Away' or 'Textease', provide a describing word on screen for the children to see in large text – for example, 'rough'. Show them how to change the font style, size and colour. Talk to them about making changes to the font to make the font match the word. For example, how can we make the word 'bendy' look bendy? If you have a projector and whiteboard show the whole class first then let them to work on the words in pairs. Print off the words and use them for a wall display describing the different materials.

The same but different

We can use describing words to compare materials. Look at the examples below. Try to complete the table. You may be able to think of some examples yourself – write them at the bottom of the table.

hard	harder	hardest
soft	softer	softest
dull	duller	dullest
shiny	shinier	shiniest
rough	rougher	roughest
bendy	bendier	bendiest
stretchy	stretchier	stretchiest
strong		
weak		
thin		
thick		
clear		
cold		
warm		
heavy		

The same but different

We can group objects in lots of different ways. We can group the five things below by the material from which they are made.

Made from plastic	Not made from plastic
ball	basket
toothbrush	golf club
pen	

We can group them by what they are used for.

Used for sport	Not used for sport
ball	basket
golf club	pen
	toothbrush

PHOTOCOPIABLE

The same but different

The same material can be used to make many different objects.

Glass

The same object can be made from many different materials.

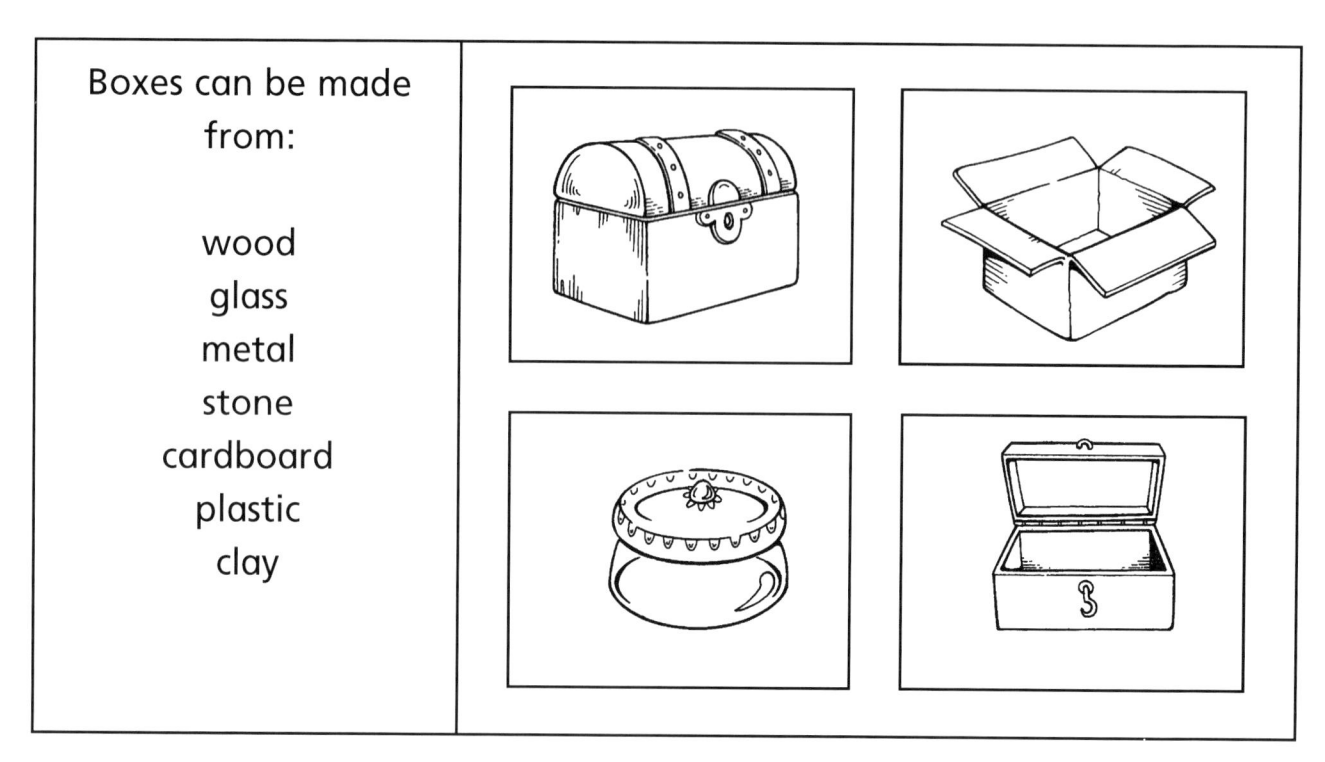

Boxes can be made from:

wood
glass
metal
stone
cardboard
plastic
clay

The same but different

4 GENERIC SHEET

PHOTOCOPIABLE

CURRICULUM FOCUS • MATERIALS 25

Name _____

The same but different

ACTIVITY SHEET 1

In the boxes stick pictures of things that can be made from plastic. Colour all the 'bendy' objects in one colour, and all the 'not bendy' objects in another colour.

	Plastic	

Some things can be made from different types of material. Use the word bank to write down materials from which cups can be made.

Cups can be made from:
_____
_____
_____

WORD BANK
metal   paper   porcelain

26 CURRICULUM FOCUS • MATERIALS

PHOTOCOPIABLE

Name _____

The same but different

ACTIVITY SHEET 2

In the 'plastic' column below, write or stick in pictures of things that can be made from plastic. In the 'metal' column write or stick in pictures of things that can be made of metal.

Plastic	Metal

Some things can be made from different types of material.
Write down four materials that cups can be made from.

_____   _____   _____   _____

Now group the objects you are given into two different groups: shiny and not shiny. On the back of this sheet, record them in a table under the labels: 'shiny' and 'not shiny'.

PHOTOCOPIABLE

CURRICULUM FOCUS • MATERIALS   27

Name _____

The same but different

ACTIVITY SHEET 3

Put the materials that your teacher gives you into two different groups: shiny and not shiny. Record your results in this table.

Shiny	Not shiny

On another sheet of paper, record other groups in other tables: hard and not hard; bendy and not bendy; rough and not rough.

Some things can be made from different types of material. Write down materials that spoons can be made from.

_____   _____   _____   _____

_____   _____   _____   _____

On the back of this sheet, make a list of all the plastic objects you might find in a kitchen.

Magnetic materials

TEACHERS' NOTES

Children have a fascination with magnets and could play with them endlessly, so it is important to guide their focus towards finding out which materials are magnetic. A more in-depth study of magnets is covered in Unit 3C 'Magnets and springs' so the emphasis here is not on the magnets themselves but on magnetic effects.

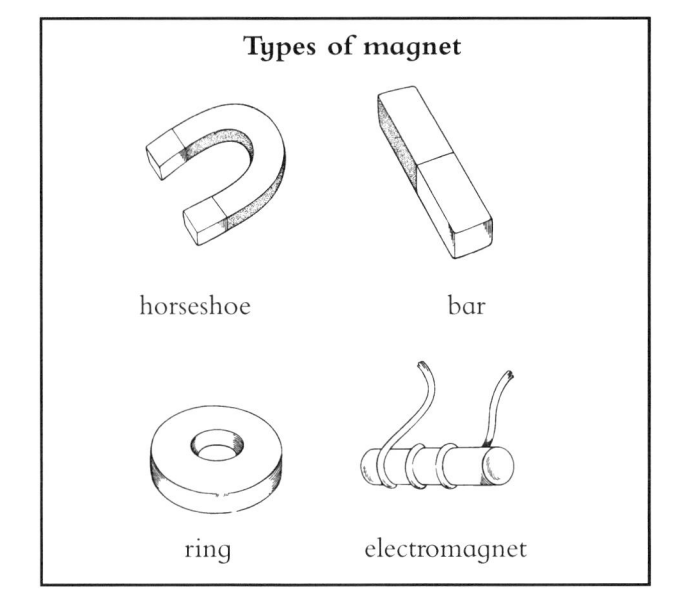

Types of magnet

horseshoe   bar

ring   electromagnet

There are two main groups of magnets – permanent magnets and electromagnets.

- Permanent magnets stay magnetic without any power supply and are usually made from steel, iron or a ceramic compound (hard and greyish black with a tendency to crack or chip). These are the familiar types of magnet that should be used in this lesson. They can vary in strength and in shape (horseshoe, bar, ring).

- Electromagnets are made from wire wrapped around a piece of metal (which can be of whatever shape suits its purpose). They require a flow of electricity to produce a magnetic effect. These are less well known, though widely used in everyday items such as food mixers, power drills and washing machines. All electric motors use magnetism and a flow of electricity to produce movement. A simple use of electromagnets that could be discussed with the class is the lifting of scrap metal such as old cars – a crane is fitted with a powerful electromagnet instead of a hook and is used to pick up steel or iron objects. Electromagnets have the advantage of being very strong and, of course, they can be switched off. Some children might recognise that when you have a magnet strong enough to pick up a car, it would be difficult to separate the magnet from the car unless the magnet can be switched off.

Magnetic materials

Only a few types of material are strongly attracted to magnets – these include the metals steel, iron, nickel and cobalt. Other materials also have magnetic properties but we can ignore these – the effects are about 1,000 times weaker than for magnetic materials and we simply class them as non-magnetic.

Steel is an alloy (a metal mixture). Steel consists of over 90 per cent iron, the remaining substances being added in various proportions to change the properties of the iron (for example, to make it stronger, springy or rust resistant). Since steel is magnetic and steel is the most common metal in everyday use, it is not surprising that children think that all metals are magnetic. It is important to obtain some non-magnetic metal samples to prove the point. Steel is used whenever an inexpensive but strong metal is required – for car bodies and engines, washing machines and other white goods, girders, cutlery, nails, nuts and bolts, machinery and so on.

Iron is a metallic element (made of only one substance) but it is not particularly strong or versatile so it is almost always mixed with other materials to make steel. Since steel is made from a very high percentage of iron, people often use the term 'iron and steel' without much regard for the difference. Metals that are iron or mostly iron are called 'ferrous'.

Nickel and cobalt are also metallic elements. They are not commonly used as pure metals but are commonly used in alloys. Nickel is one of the many metals that are put into the alloy mixes for coins – one American coin is called the 'nickel'. Some UK coins contain enough nickel to make them magnetic; some do not – this can surprise children.

Non-magnetic materials

Apart from steel and iron just about everything else in everyday life can be classed as non-magnetic, so there is no shortage of non-magnetic examples – glass, plastic, wood, stone and so on. Common metals that are non-magnetic are copper, aluminium and copper-based alloys such as brass. Bicycle frames and wheels are often made of steel but better quality ones (because they are lighter) may be made of aluminium alloys or even more expensive non-magnetic materials like carbon fibre or magnesium. Even though we can't see because of the surface paint, a magnet can be used to tell the difference.

Tin and tin cans

Tin is a non-magnetic metal but the so-called 'tin can' of beans or soup is really a steel can with a very thin coating of tin. Tin cans are attracted to a magnet because of the steel and not because of the tin. Tin does not rust so steel cans are coated with it to ensure the steel does not rust and contaminate the food. (Some people avoid buying dented cans because the tin coating might be damaged and the steel could be rusting inside.)

Recycling

Some cans are made of aluminium (look for the recycling label 'ALU' on the can). This is a much more expensive metal than steel. Recycling points often ask for steel and aluminium cans to be put into separate collection bins and some councils provide magnets to check which type of can you have since the aluminium ones are non-magnetic. This could be a useful class exercise and a practical application of their newly acquired knowledge. But beware – sometimes aluminium examples are quite difficult to find.

Making use of magnets

The compass is the simplest and oldest device that uses magnetic materials. Originally, a naturally occurring magnet called lodestone (a type of rock) was suspended or floated so that it could turn to point north. Compass needles are now made of steel. Steel can be magnetised by putting it close to a strong magnet. Certain types of steel will stay magnetic for a long time.

Electric motors, loudspeakers and some security switches make use of magnets though these are well hidden in their internal workings.

Fridge magnets and those incorporated into a wide variety of toys are more obvious examples for children. Fridge doors usually have a magnet built into the rubber strip that seals the door. This holds the door shut.

Medical scanning makes use of extremely strong magnetic fields in MRI (magnetic resonance imaging). This makes use of the fact that all materials are affected by magnetic fields, to build up a picture of the inside of the human body.

Shards of steel have been removed from patients' eyes (after violent explosions) by drawing them out with powerful magnets.

Recycling metals – to separate iron and steel from other metals a powerful electromagnet is waved over them. The magnet will lift the iron and steel and the other metals will be left behind.

Metal detectors use a magnetic field to detect metal objects in the ground. They have a discriminator control that helps to tell the difference between iron and more valuable silver and gold. Airport security metal detectors work in a similar way.

Watch out!

Credit cards/cash cards have a black magnetic strip that holds coded information. If you place this near to a magnet – for example, on top of a loudspeaker – you risk wiping the magnetic code and being left unable to use the card.

Colour television screens and PC monitors have a metal mask just behind the glass screen. If this is made from steel and a magnet is brought near, it can become magnetised, causing the colours to be distorted and producing some weird effects. It is not advisable to try this as the effect may be permanent and require the services of a television repair company to remove it. It is up to the teacher to judge whether to disclose this information – it may be wiser just to ensure that magnet activities are conducted well away from these items than to tempt children who will inevitably be curious to see what happens.

Vocabulary

Alloy A mix of two or more metals – for example, brass is a mix of zinc and copper.

Attraction Pulling of (unlike) magnetic poles to each other.

Electromagnet A magnet that uses a flow of electricity through a coil of wire to produce magnetism. When the electricity is cut off, the electromagnet stops working.

Ferrous Metal that contains a significant amount of iron – for example, steel is ferrous.

Iron An element (made of only one substance); a common metal that is magnetic.

Magnet Anything that causes magnetic attraction (or repulsion).

Magnetic Any material attracted to a magnet.

Non-magnetic Any material that is not attracted to a magnet.

Permanent magnet A magnet that stays magnetic; its magnetism comes from the materials it is made from.

Poles Magnets have north and south poles. North poles repel north poles, south poles repel south poles, but north and south poles attract each other.

Repulsion Pushing away of (like) magnetic poles.

Steel An alloy that consists mostly of iron and is magnetic.

Magnetic materials	Non-magnetic materials
iron steel cobalt nickel	plastic (all types) wood (and paper) cotton (and other natural fibres) glass (and most ceramics) stone (except for unusual ores containing iron) tin brass aluminium copper lead zinc silver gold

CURRICULUM FOCUS • MATERIALS

Magnetic materials

Science objectives (Unit 1C)
- To know that some materials are magnetic but most are not.
- To think about which objects they expect to be attracted to a magnet.
- To make observations, communicate what happened, and with help, use results to draw conclusions saying whether their predictions were right.

Resources

- Magnets, including a horseshoe magnet and a bar magnet
- A general selection of objects that are magnetic and non-magnetic (see the table on page 31) and some sample materials labelled with the type of material
- A specific selection of objects as shown on Activity sheets 1, 2 and 3 – comb, fork, mug, trainer, bottle top, paper-clip, ruler, hairbrush, 10p coin, T-shirt, spanner, pencil, pen with metal clip, book, can, wire, 2p coin (one set for each group)
- Generic sheets 1–4 (pages 34–37)
- Activity sheets 1–3 (pages 38–40)

Safety issues

- Magnets can damage television screens and computer monitors.
- Avoid sharp objects such as nails.
- Avoid iron filings (sometimes used in experiments with magnets but an irritant especially to the eyes).

Starting points: *whole class*

Show the horseshoe magnet and ask the children if they recognise it (a red painted horseshoe magnet is most readily recognised). Discuss other magnet shapes and some of their uses. Use Generic sheets 1 and 2 here (perhaps enlarged on an OHP). The children are likely to be aware of the simpler examples, such as fridge magnets.

Appropriate questions are:

- Does anyone know what this is?
- What can you do with it?
- What could it be used for?
- Have you seen or used any magnets?
- Which things around us use magnets?

With one steel object and one plastic object, ask the children to predict what will happen when you put a magnet near each one. Before testing the objects with the magnet, it is important to emphasise the process of predicting the result, then checking and finally discussing the outcome. Emphasise this sequence by using Generic sheet 3.

Let the children test materials to see if they are magnetic. Encourage them to predict first.

Predictions: important issues

Predicting should involve thinking rather than a wild guess but until a child has some related experience (in or out of the class) then it will inevitably be guesswork. Predicting may be a bit of a challenge but it is very important that it is seen as fun. If the prediction does not match the result it must not be seen as a failure but instead should be seen as an opportunity to improve understanding and lead to more reliable predictions.

Predicting should enhance the depth with which the children think, help them to recognise patterns and eventually, in future topics, lead to conclusions. Some children will be unsure and require support both at the predicting and the discussion stages. For example, when a group is testing a variety of objects, they may come up with the following:

Prediction: 'The magnet will pick up the aluminium foil.'

Check: 'The magnet doesn't pick up the foil.'

Discuss: 'Perhaps magnets don't pick up all types of metal.'

Group activities

Activity sheet 1

This sheet is aimed at children who are capable of understanding which objects are magnetic but find it difficult to relate the magnetism to the material. They should predict, check and discuss within their groups their findings on the testing of which objects are magnetic. They may notice a pattern in the materials from which magnetic objects are made.

Activity sheet 2

This sheet is aimed at children of average ability who are able to recognise which materials are magnetic. They should predict, check and discuss within their groups their findings on the testing of which materials are magnetic. They should give some examples of materials (not objects) that are magnetic and non-magnetic and put the results in a table.

Activity sheet 3

This sheet is aimed at more able children who are able to recognise which materials are magnetic and to apply this knowledge to possible uses of the materials. They should predict, check and discuss within their groups their findings on the testing of which materials are magnetic. They should give some examples of materials (not objects) that are and are not magnetic and put the results in a table. They should make a statement or explain how or where it might be important whether materials are magnetic or non-magnetic.

Plenary session

Use a magnet to explore a bicycle. Give out copies of Generic sheet 4 and ask the children to predict which parts are magnetic and colour them in on the top picture. They should then test their theories on a real bicycle and record the results on the bottom picture. Discuss with the whole class ideas such as expected results versus actual and how magnetism works even when the metal has been painted.

Ideas for support

Create a display of magnetic and non-magnetic materials.

Produce a giant magnet poster. Draw a large magnet at the top. Cut out pictures of different objects from magazines and get the children to stick those pictures that are of magnetic objects to the magnet and those that aren't at the bottom of the poster as if they had fallen off the magnet. Each object could be labelled.

Ideas for extension

Challenge: how to find a needle in a haystack. Tell the children about the problem and see if they can suggest an easy way to solve it. You could set up a similar experiment (without needles) – for example, find a paper-clip that has fallen into some pencil shavings or a key that has dropped into a dark liquid (some ink or paint in water).

Linked ICT activities

Use the Roamer or other similar remote control toys. Place about ten metallic and non metallic objects with which the children will be familiar, on a numberline (up to ten) vertically in front of you. If you are using the Roamer make a long numberline out of A4 sheets by sticking them together lengthways. This will help when you use the Roamer as, when it moves forward one unit, it moves forward the length of one sheet of A4 paper.

Provide cards with either the word 'metallic' or 'non-metalic' written on the them. They place the cards face-down in front of the number line.

The objective of the activity is to program the Roamer to move forwards and backwards along the number line to stop by a card. The child turns over the card and whatever it says, they program the Roamer to move to the nearest metallic or non-metallic object. This activity could either be carried out in pairs, small groups or with the whole class.

Magnetic materials

Magnets come in different shapes and sizes.

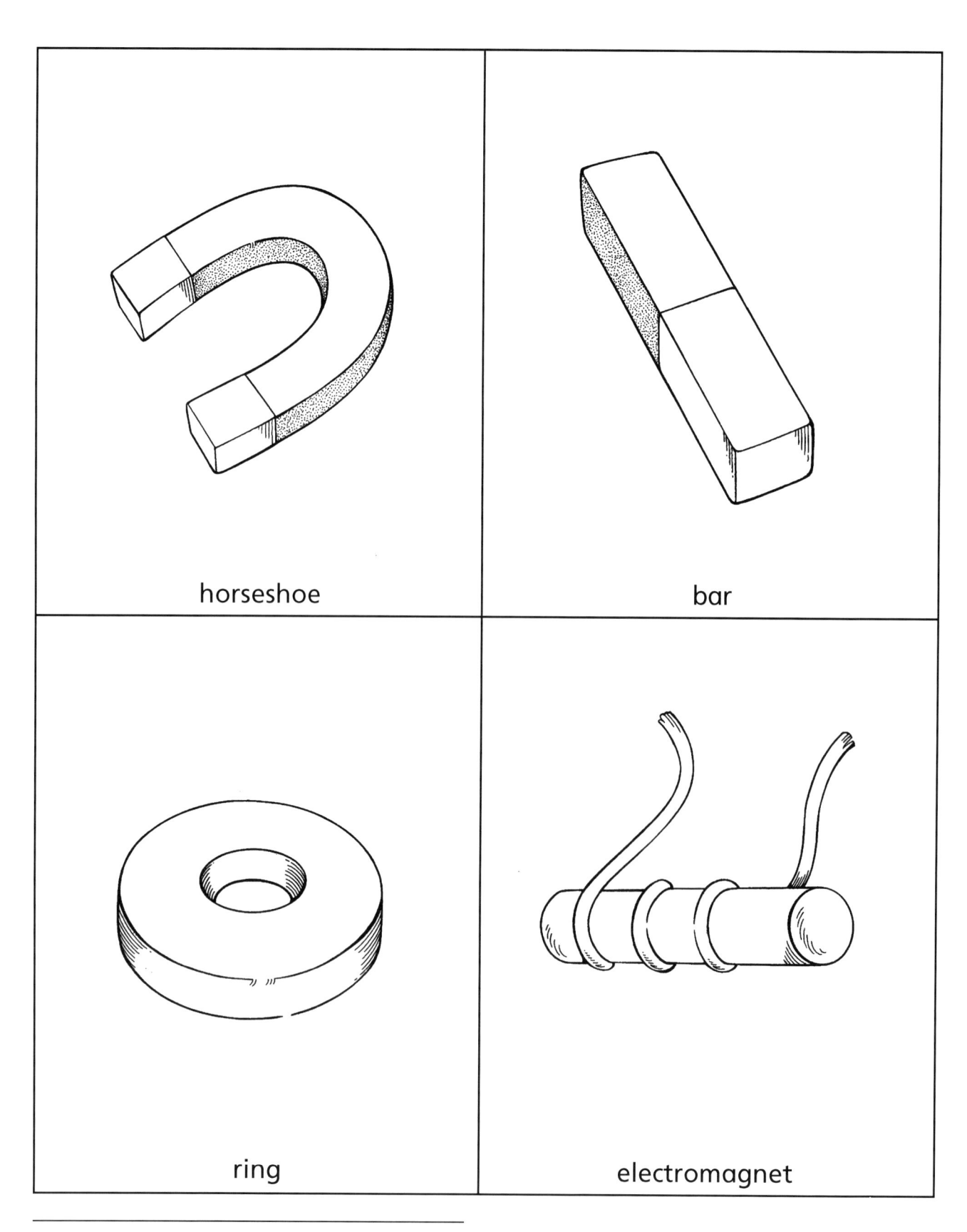

horseshoe	bar
ring	electromagnet

Magnetic materials

Things that use magnets

fridge magnet	burglar alarm switch
compass	fridge door
washing machine	electric motor

GENERIC SHEET 3

Magnetic materials

Predict

Try to guess what will happen.

Check

Check it out to see if your prediction matches what happens.

Discuss

Have a chat about it.

Did your prediction match what happened?

Have you a better idea about what to predict next time?

Magnetic materials

4 GENERIC SHEET

Predict
Colour in the parts of the bike that you think are magnetic.

Now use a magnet to test the parts of a real bike. Colour in the parts that are magnetic.

PHOTOCOPIABLE

CURRICULUM FOCUS • MATERIALS 37

Name _____

Magnetic materials

ACTIVITY SHEET 1

Predict

Draw a line to connect the magnet to each object that you think is magnetic.

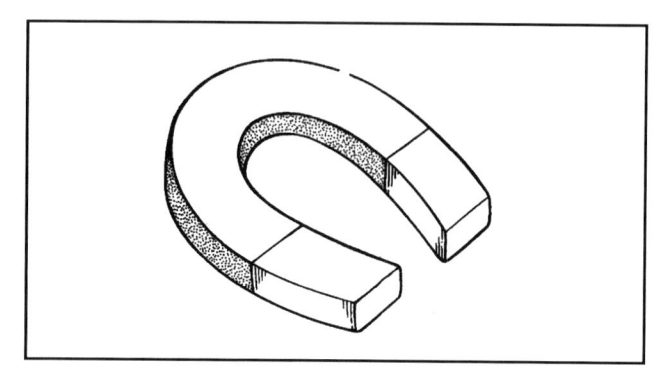

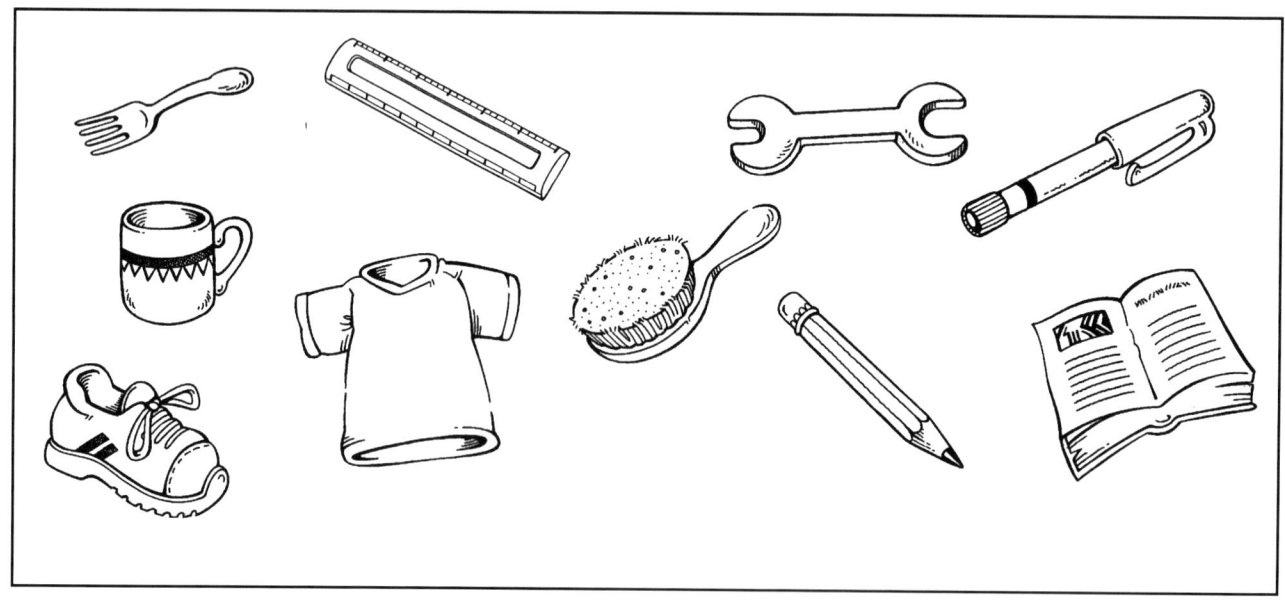

Check

Use a magnet on the real objects to check if you are right.

Discuss

Do you notice anything about the objects that are attracted to the magnet?

Now predict and test to see if some other objects are magnetic.
Draw a picture of a magnet and these new objects on another sheet.
Draw a line to connect any magnetic ones to the magnet.

38 CURRICULUM FOCUS • MATERIALS

PHOTOCOPIABLE

Name _____

Magnetic materials

ACTIVITY SHEET 2

Predict
Draw a line to connect the magnet to each object that you think is magnetic.

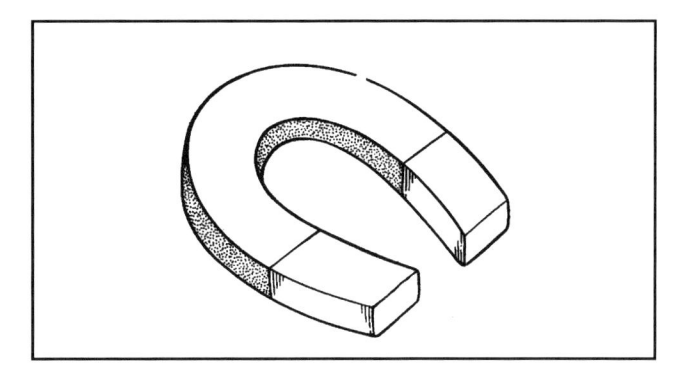

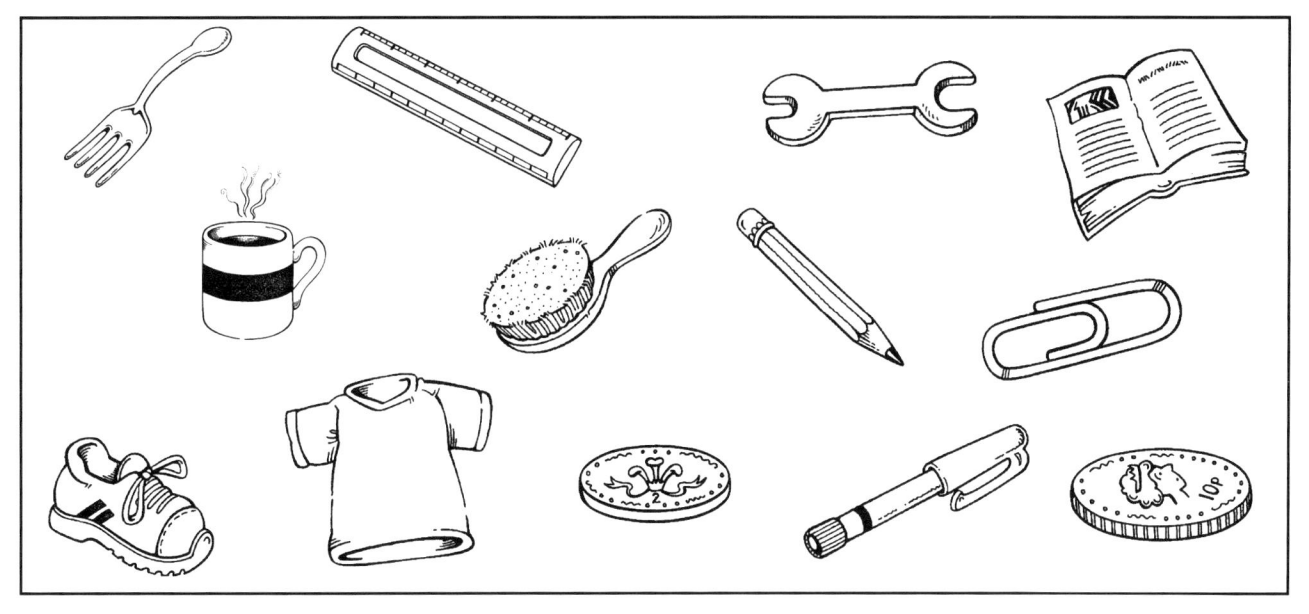

Check
Use a magnet on the real objects to check if you are right.

Discuss
Write down what you notice about the types of material that are attracted to the magnet.

Now check your idea about which types of material are magnetic by testing some other objects. On another sheet, draw a table of the objects with two headings: 'magnetic materials' and 'non-magnetic materials'.

PHOTOCOPIABLE

CURRICULUM FOCUS • MATERIALS 39

Name _____

Magnetic materials

ACTIVITY SHEET 3

Predict
Draw lines to connect the magnet to the objects that you think are magnetic.

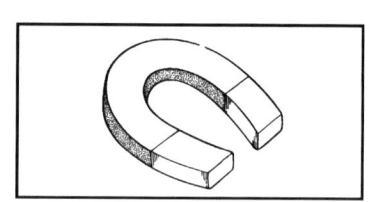

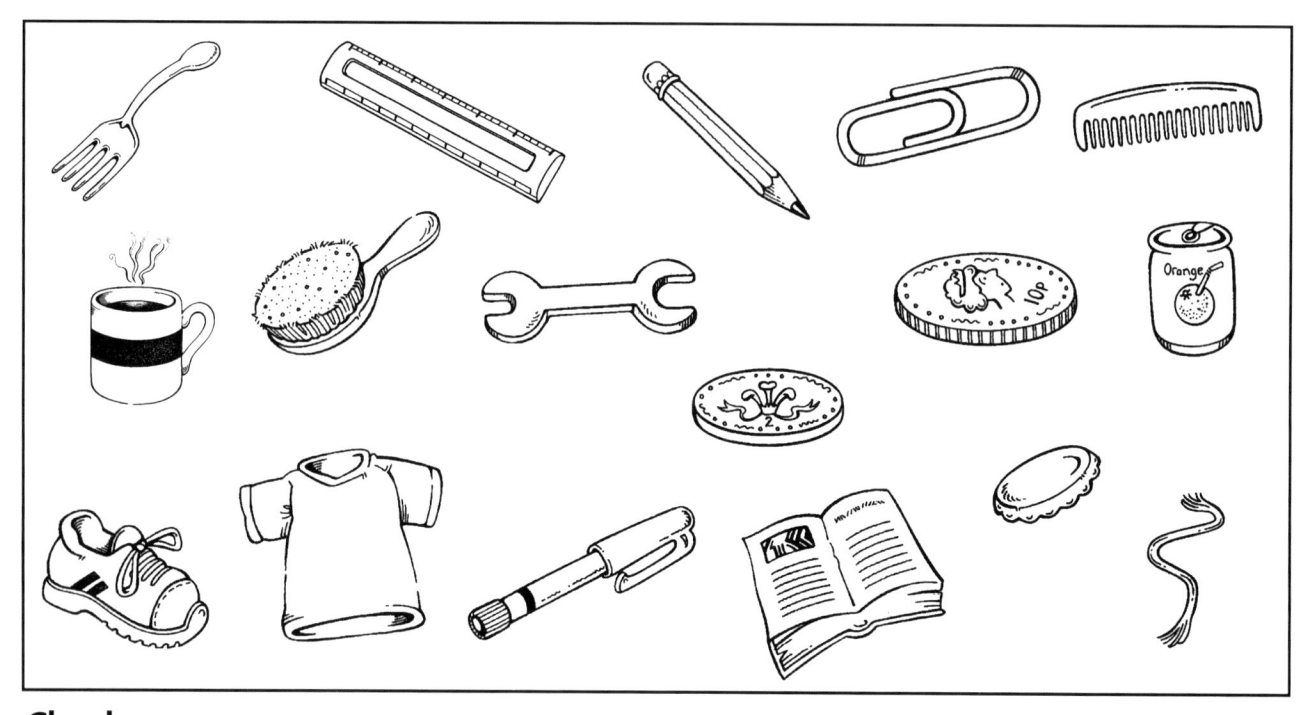

Check
Use a magnet on the real objects to check if you are right.

Discuss
Write down what you notice about the types of material that are attracted to the magnet.

Results
Check your idea about which types of material are magnetic by testing some other objects.

On another sheet, draw up a table of the objects under two headings: 'magnetic materials' and 'non-magnetic materials'.
Discuss why being magnetic can be important for an object. On the back of this sheet, write two sentences about your ideas.

Material pick 'n' mix

TEACHERS' NOTES

The best material for the job

The question of which material is best for the job can be tackled at a very basic level. There are some obvious examples, such as glass being used for a windowpane because it is clear. This particular example is straightforward because the most important property – being clear – is not all that common in other materials. At the simplest level we can say that each object is made from the material with the best properties. It might be possible to hand pick a set of simple examples like this but, as ever, real life is not quite so straightforward.

Many materials for the job

Objects are commonly made from more than one material – for example, a pen may have a plastic barrel, a rubber grip and a metal tip. This is not really a problem because the function of each part can be examined and its purpose explained – for example, the grip is rubber because it is soft and, therefore, comfortable to hold; the tip is made from metal because it is smooth and tough to glide across the paper; and the barrel is often plastic because it is light and inexpensive and can easily be moulded into shape.

In Chapter 2, children looked at collections in which there were samples of the same type of object made from different materials – for example, a cup can be made from plastic, (waxed) paper, metal and clay (ceramic). Despite the different properties of these materials they are still suitable for a broadly similar task. To understand why, it is important to identify what the essential properties are. Since cups are used to hold liquids they have to be both waterproof and strong enough to keep their shape. Other properties of a cup may be desirable but they depend on the particular situation in which they are used – for example, plastic and metal cups are used for camping because they are tough and less likely to be damaged. Even in the camping context there is a choice to make – plastic cups are lighter, which is an advantage for backpackers, but metal ones won't melt if heated on a campfire.

More inquisitive and observant children may start to notice and ask questions about the variety of materials that can be used for the same object. Clearly one reason for a variety of materials being used is that varying conditions and circumstances can make one material more suitable than another. This means that the 'best' material often depends on how it is going to be used and not just on its form – a concept that children with more insight should be able to appreciate. There are often other factors that influence the material used.

Properties that matter

When talking about the best material for a job, encourage the children to use the list of properties in earlier chapters – with some additions, such as waterproof (to be investigated in Chapter 5) and wear-resistant.

Other things that matter

Even though children are asked to consider the suitability of materials based on how their properties affect their usage, other important factors to be aware of are:

- cost of the raw material and cost of manufacture
- availability
- personal preferences/fashion
- environmental factors
- manufacturing processes.

The first three are fairly obvious. Environmental issues such as deforestation, chemical hazards (such as oil spills and pollution during production) and the ability to be recycled ought to be taken into consideration when choosing materials. This will probably become more of an issue as more value is put on the environment and finite resources become scarcer.

Manufacturing issues can be extremely important. Some materials are chosen not because they give any advantage in the final product, but because the manufacturer finds them easier to use in the production process. Plastic is one of the most widely used materials – this is partly due to the ease with which it can be poured into moulds to make any required shape.

From what to why

Children can often say what material should be used but not why. They might, for example, state that metal is good for making saucepans but be unsure why it is suitable. They may also be able to identify the properties of the metal but find it difficult to identify which of the many properties are the important ones. The metal being shiny or having a metallic appearance does not really matter too much, but the facts that it is a good conductor of heat and does not melt on the stove are vitally important. The pick 'n' mix game is designed to help children become more analytical about the use of materials. The game is light-hearted but nevertheless takes the children beyond recognising suitable materials to question and hopefully understand how properties make materials suitable. Explaining why a material is appropriate requires a deeper level of thinking that is worth attempting, but one that some children may find challenging.

How deep to go?

Some more able children will weigh up several properties and give a reasoned explanation for a material's suitability. Others may only manage the simplest and most obvious examples. These ranges are covered in the activity sheets. Be prepared – children meet materials all the time and may well ask questions requiring an answer beyond this coverage of the topic. For example, the children may ask why plastic cups are used in vending machines. This is because of the low cost and also the manufacturer's ability to make the cups thin enough to stack. Neither of these can be explained simply in terms of properties.

Material pick 'n' mix

Science objective (Unit 1C)
- To know that materials are chosen for specific purposes on the basis of their properties.

Resources

- Pick 'n' mix games, one for demonstration to the whole class and others for each group of children during the activities. You need either the spinner on Generic sheet 1 (better for whole-class work) or a dice and the cards on Generic sheet 2 (for group work), plus the picture cards on Generic sheets 3 and 4
- A displayed list of the materials' names
- A display of the words used to describe materials
- A few sample objects – for example, a ceramic cup, a metal spoon, a rubber ball, a jar and a sock
- Generic sheets 1–4 (pages 46–49)
- Activity sheets 1–3 (pages 50–52)

Starting points: *whole class*

Spend five to ten minutes revising materials and their properties.

Remind the children of the wide range of materials that we use by asking them to identify some around the classroom and pointing them out on the list of 'names of materials'.

Remind them of some of the characteristics of materials (but not all, unless it becomes apparent that a thorough revision is necessary). Ask them to choose words that match materials in the classroom. Indicate the 'words used to describe materials' display, which will help them.

Now show them the sample objects and tell them that they are going to try to work out why these things have been made from these materials. Take one object at a time and discuss its function, the properties of the material and why these properties are suited to this function.

Ask questions such as:

- What is this?
- What is it used for?
- What is it made from?
- What words do we use to describe this material? (What are its properties/characteristics?)
- Why has it been made from this material?

Repeat for a few objects, helping the children to focus on the relevance of the material's properties to how the object is used.

Now play the Pick 'n' mix game. The game can be made in two versions. The first is better for demonstration and consists of a spinner board and a set of picture cards (see Generic sheets 1–4 for templates – the spinner board would be best enlarged to A3/A2 size to be more visible).

How to play
1. Shuffle the cards (made from Generic sheets 3 and 4) and place them face down.
2. Twirl the spinner so that when the arrow comes to rest it points to a material – for example, rubber.
3. Ask a child to pick up the top card from the pile. This card gives a picture of an object – for example, a fork.
4. Ask the child to decide if the material on the spinner board is suitable for making the object on the card they are holding. For example, is rubber suitable for making a fork?
5. The child should give their reasons.
6. If the reasons are acceptable, that child is next to twirl the spinner.

For a group of children, the non-spinner version of the game needs just an ordinary dice, the cards from Generic sheet 2 and the object cards from Generic sheets 3 and 4. A child rolls the dice and the number determines which material is to be matched with an object card (see Generic sheet 2).

Obviously, there may be a good number of unsuitable material–object matches during the game – this is an important and intentional feature. It is just as valid and thought provoking to explain why a material is unsuitable, as it is to explain why another might be suitable.

Decide how long to play the game, bearing in mind that the children need to have a good idea of the process if they are going to be asked to play the game in the group activity. Also, they need to meet new combinations when they play the game in groups.

Group activities

Activity sheet 1
This sheet is aimed at children who can recognise basic material types and identify at least one of the main properties of these materials. In the first part of the activity they complete an exercise where just one appropriate property, chosen from a word bank, has to be selected.

Then they have to complete sentences to say why objects should not be made from a particular material. Encourage them to choose words from the 'words used to describe materials' display, because they will often give explanations involving what would happen rather than what property makes it unsuitable – for example, 'Because it would break,' rather than 'Because it is not tough.' Such explanations aren't wrong, but it is important to focus on how the properties match the function rather than on events that might occur if a particular material were used.

Activity sheet 2
This sheet is aimed at children who know a fair range of material types and know several of their properties. In the first part of the activity the children are asked to complete an object/material/ properties exercise and record two properties for each example. Then they complete sentences about suitable and unsuitable materials, ending with two sentences where they decide which materials would not be suitable for the specified object.

Activity sheet 3
This sheet is aimed at children who can recognise a fair range of material types and know the main properties of these materials. They choose given objects and write sentences to say what the objects should be made from, and why. Next they should write what the objects should not be made from, and why. Then they choose an object of their own and write about it.

Plenary session

Hold a question and answer session.

- Why do we sometimes use paper bags and at other times plastic bags?
- Why are some bottles plastic and some glass?
- What are the advantages and disadvantages of a glass-topped table?
- Why are toy tools made from plastic when real ones are mostly metal?
- Garden furniture made from plastic is light. Why is being light both an advantage and a disadvantage?

Ideas for support

In the introduction to the lesson, some large display-type examples could be built up. For example, begin with a poster-sized picture of a cup. Add a label to say what it is made from (getting the class to suggest a suitable material), then add labels describing the material's properties (again with suggested properties from the class). Finally, identify through discussion the most important properties and highlight them or put them at the top of the poster to show their merit. Some displays of this type could be left up for children to consult during the activities.

Ideas for extension

Use the ideas from the pick 'n' mix game to generate posters showing stupid material choices and smart material choices.

Do a survey of pens, pencils and rulers in the class (or choose other items) to find out how many are made of each type of material. As a follow up discuss the advantages and disadvantages of the different materials.

Design something – for example, a car, house, kitchenware – and label it with appropriate materials.

Do some research into special materials being used for special purposes – for example, carbon fibre in racing cars, titanium in darts, tungsten carbide in drill tips, diamonds in jewellery and in stone cutting blades.

Linked ICT activities

Using 'Talking Write Away', 'Teaxtease', 'Clicker 4' or any other similar program that allows you to create wordbanks, create a bank of words that the children have become familiar with that are associated with materials. Write the name of an object on the screen and ask the children to select words from the wordbank that could be used to describe the object. Add the words to the page. Print out the word with the descriptions and place the print out next to the object to create a display of words used to describe different objects.

1 GENERIC SHEET

Material pick 'n' mix

The pick 'n' mix game

Fix a copy of the disc onto heavy card or a notice board. Cut out the arrow and stick it onto card. Find the central point of the arrow by balancing it on a pin. Fix the arrow through its central point with a tack so that it can spin freely to point randomly to materials. To adjust the balance of the arrow, add paper-clips.

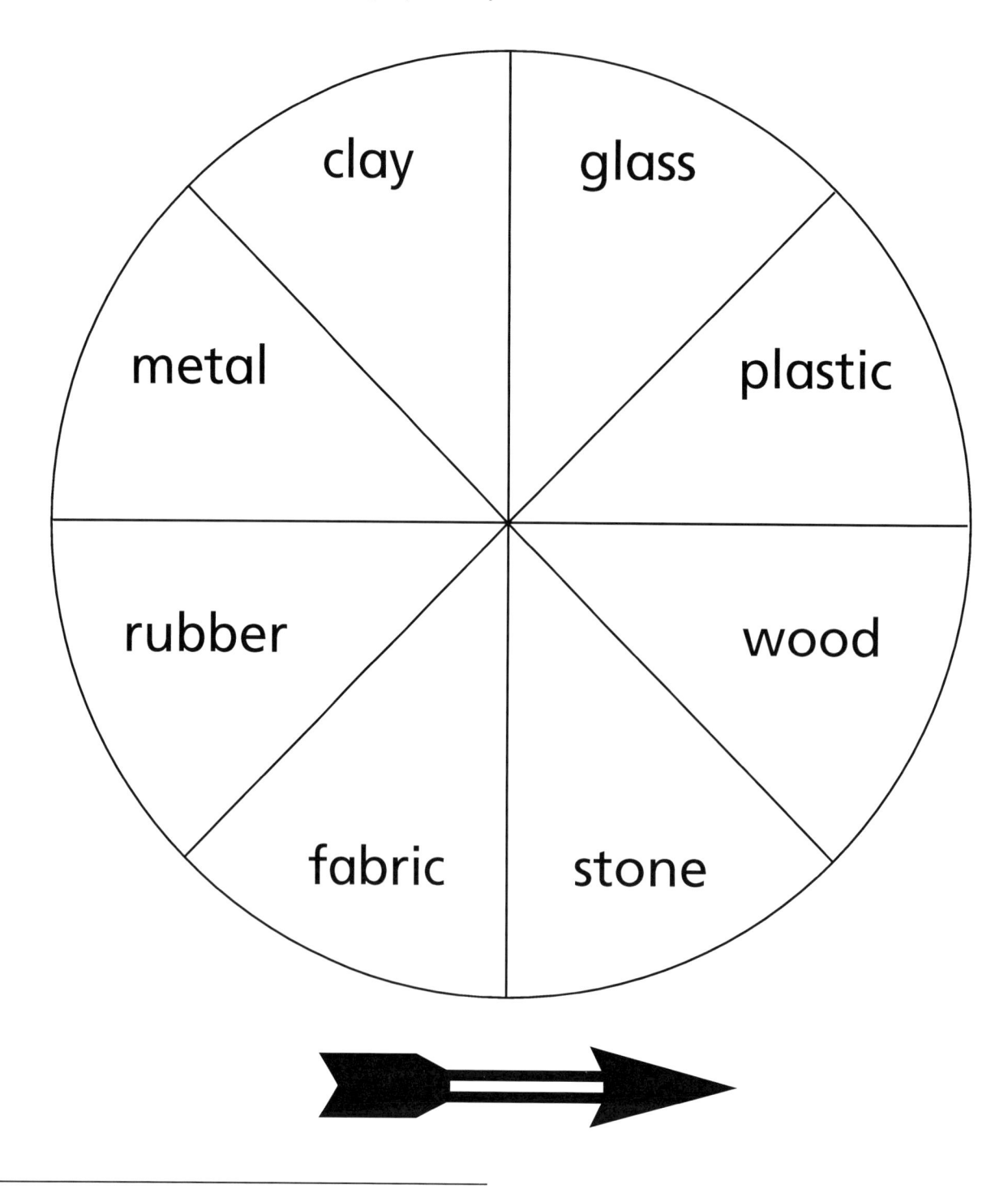

- clay
- glass
- metal
- plastic
- rubber
- wood
- fabric
- stone

CURRICULUM FOCUS • MATERIALS

PHOTOCOPIABLE

Material pick 'n' mix

2 GENERIC SHEET

Throw the dice. The number on top says which material to use.

⚀	plastic	⚁	wood
⚂	metal	⚃	clay
⚄	glass	⚅	rubber

Material pick 'n' mix

Cut out the pictures and stick them onto card.

48 CURRICULUM FOCUS • MATERIALS

PHOTOCOPIABLE

Material pick 'n' mix

Cut out the pictures and stick them onto card.

PHOTOCOPIABLE

CURRICULUM FOCUS • MATERIALS

Name _____

Material pick 'n' mix

ACTIVITY SHEET 1

Choose one word from the word bank to complete each sentence.

WORD BANK
rough   shiny   hard   stretchy   strong
bouncy   clear   heavy   tough   waterproof

A nail	is made from **metal**	because it needs to be _____
A tyre	is made from **rubber**	because it needs to be _____
A window	is made from **glass**	because it needs to be _____

Complete the sentences below.

A spoon	should not be made from **paper**	because it would _____
A kite	should not be made from **metal**	because it would _____
A window	should not be made from **wood**	because it needs to be _____

50 CURRICULUM FOCUS • MATERIALS

PHOTOCOPIABLE

Name _____

Material pick 'n' mix

ACTIVITY SHEET 2

Use the word bank to put two words in each box.

WORD BANK
rough   shiny   hard   stretchy   strong
bouncy   clear   heavy   tough   waterproof

A nail	is made from **metal**	because it needs to be _____ and _____
A tyre	is made from **rubber**	because it needs to be _____ and _____
A window	is made from **glass**	because it needs to be _____ and _____

Complete the sentences below.

1. A nail should not be made from glass because _____

2. A window should not be made from wood because _____

3. A kite is made from paper because _____

4. A kite should not be made from _____ because _____

5. A chair should not be made from _____ because _____

PHOTOCOPIABLE

CURRICULUM FOCUS • MATERIALS 51

Name _____

Material pick 'n' mix

ACTIVITY SHEET 3

Choose three objects from the box. On another sheet of paper write sentences to say what they should be made from, and why.

For the same three objects, write three sentences saying what they should not be made from, and why.

Now choose an object of your own and write about it.

52   CURRICULUM FOCUS • MATERIALS   PHOTOCOPIABLE

Materials put to the test

CHAPTER 5

TEACHERS' NOTES

Measurement versus opinion

In their previous work on materials children have used their senses (possibly also some additional resources) and have recorded their observations in an imprecise way – for example, they may have stated that a material is hard or bendy.

It is important to acknowledge that these observations are based on judgement and that human judgement is unreliable. A person's judgement may vary from day to day, be affected by circumstances or depend on criteria that may be different from person to person. Take, for example, a situation where three people are asked about how hot it was in a sauna. One might tell us it was too hot, another that it was pleasantly warm and another that it was 30°C. The first two are matters of opinion, the third a measurement. It is clear that the measurement is a more useful and reliable way to express the information.

Observations that involve measurement, such as 'The temperature is 25°C,' are called 'quantitative'. Observations that involve comparison, such as 'This material is hard, the other is soft,' are called 'qualitative'. Children do not need to know this terminology but it is important that where possible they begin to move from opinions towards more reliable measurements. This will involve building up measurement skills and developing the ability to both measure and record quantitative information. These skills will be acquired through gradual exposure. This chapter provides an opportunity to practise such skills. However, for children who are not ready, it is perfectly possible to complete the activity by observing and making comparisons rather than by taking measurements.

Early experiments

This will be one of the first science experiments that involves the children going beyond just making observations. They must devise a method and use some equipment in order to do testing.

Experiments are fundamental to modern science. The Ancient Greeks were very advanced in their thinking, excelling in philosophy, mathematics and the arts. However, their progress in science was haphazard because they did not test their scientific ideas with experiments. Sometimes their ideas were right and sometimes they were wrong, but without experiments they were unable to tell which was which.

There are many ways in which knowledge is acquired. Children experiment naturally with things around them in an informal, 'Let's try this out,' kind of way. They learn by exploring, watching others, working things out, finding things out by accident and by using trial and error methods. So, too, scientific discoveries can be made in many different ways.

Here we are introducing one of the most common methods. If the concept of doing an experiment is new to the children then the idea of what an experiment is will need to be introduced. An experiment can be described as a way to check out ideas by testing, although a fuller idea will be gained by leading them gently through the scientific steps (described below).

Steps in doing an experiment

It is not appropriate or necessary at this stage to be too rigorous about scientific procedures, to know the headings of the steps below or to write up full reports. It is necessary, however, to cover the ideas in each of the steps (some may be covered in whole-class work, some as group work – see the lesson plan on pages 55–57).

The basic scientific experiment involves the following parts:

- **Aim**. This is the purpose of the experiment – for example, the aim is to find out which materials are waterproof. There may also be a hypothesis, a scientific guess, about what the expected outcome will be.
- **Method**. This is how the experiment is carried out. It will normally include selecting equipment, deciding on the procedure considering how to keep the experiment fair.

- **Results**. This is a record of what happened and can be in many forms:
  - a few words to describe an observation.
  - a list of words put in order (for example, materials listed from hardest to softest)
  - a table containing descriptive words and/or sets of measurements
  - a graph or chart representing the results
  - a drawing/photo to show what happened
  - a sample of something to show the result – for example, dried leaves fixed to a chart showing change in colour from summer to autumn
  - other forms (they should provide a record of what happened).

- **Conclusion**. This is a statement or two to sum up what has been learned. The conclusion should be a response to the aim, saying something about what was found out but not just repeating the results – for example, 'We found that only two materials were waterproof – these were the red nylon one and the grey PVC material.' A more advanced conclusion might go on to say how this information could be useful in real life or mention something about extending the experiment, improving it or commenting on something extra that was understood or thoughts that were triggered by doing the experiment.

Materials to choose for testing

Waterproof materials. Many materials are waterproof when in the solid or sheet form. However, when made into a fibre and woven into fabric, the same material may not be waterproof as the water is usually able to seep through the weave of the fabric. Most fabrics are made waterproof by processing the fabric – for example, by coating it with water-repellent substances. It is very difficult to tell whether a fabric is waterproof just by looking at it.

Surface tension. Some materials, especially finely woven ones, may hold back liquid due to an effect known as surface tension. This is a kind of attraction that makes water stick together, as can be seen in the way that water droplets form blobs. As far as waterproofing is concerned, this can mean that water will get through the fabric but will stick to the underside without dripping off so that a suspended piece of material, as in the test, may seem to be waterproof when it isn't. One way to overcome this in an improved version of the experiment would be to have something touching the wet underside of the fabric so that the water can escape by flowing down it. See Umbrellas and tents below for more on this effect.

Sample fabrics. It is important to provide the children with a range of materials for testing, ranging from porous to waterproof. Fabrics used in most everyday clothing (such as cotton, nylon and polyester) are normally quite porous whilst fabrics designed for use as outer layers in outdoor pursuits may be waterproof (check the label). Water-resistant or shower-proof usually indicates that the material has some resistance to water penetration but will only hold it back for a limited time. It may be possible to get samples from discarded clothing; waterproofs generally leak at the seams and at high wear points before the rest of the fabric has lost its ability to repel water.

Real clothing. If clothing does not have a lining then it is possible to test it without cutting a sample – just use a convenient, unobstructed patch of the clothing, such as the tail of a jacket, and fix it across the jar for the test. Children like to do tests on real clothing, such as their jackets, but permission may be required from parents and allowances made for the fact that the tested clothing may become wet and unsuitable for wearing until dried.

Umbrellas and tents. It is suggested in the Scheme of Work learning outcomes that an umbrella needs to be waterproof. Strictly speaking, this is not true and many (perhaps most) umbrellas are not made of waterproof material. When water falls on a material that is suspended and sloping reasonably steeply, such as the curved dome of an umbrella, the water soaks into and flows along the curve rather than dripping from it. It may seem strange, but the inner surface of a non-waterproof umbrella may be soaking wet yet still function perfectly. If, however, you were to wear a jacket of this same material there would be problems. When the wet inner surface of the material touched your clothes, the water would flow onto them and you would get pretty soggy. Tents that have a fly sheet (separate outer sheet) are like the umbrella in that the material does not have to be waterproof; it does not touch the inner section of the tent but allows water to flow down and drip from the ends of the sheet onto the ground.

Materials put to the test

Science objectives (Unit 1C)
- To suggest how to test whether materials are waterproof.
- To explore ways of answering the question.
- To communicate what they did and what happened, making simple comparisons.
- To use what happened to draw a conclusion and to say what they found out.
- To suggest how to test an idea about whether a fabric or paper is suitable for a particular purpose.

Resources

- Fabrics for testing, ranging from totally non-waterproof to waterproof (see teachers' notes for further advice)
- Wide-necked, transparent containers, such as jamjars
- Elastic bands or devices for fastening fabric across the neck of the jamjar
- Water, a means for distributing it to groups and a means for wiping up or containing spills
- Devices for measuring small standardised volumes of water, such as lemonade bottle tops
- Clock with a second hand for measuring two-minute time intervals, or a two-minute timer
- Generic sheet 1 (page 58)
- Activity sheets 1-3 (pages 59–61)

Starting points: *whole class*

Introduce the idea of what is meant by the term 'waterproof' and then go on to discuss how we can tell whether or not a fabric is waterproof and how we might test it.

As you discuss this with the class, keep in mind the steps described in the teachers' notes. Use Generic sheet 1 as appropriate. Some suggestions are made for each of the steps.

- **Aim** – the purpose of the experiment. Tell the class that you want them to predict and then find out which fabrics are waterproof. Show them some fabrics and ask them which they expect to be waterproof.

- **Method** – this is how the experiment is carried out. You don't need to cover every aspect of the experiment in a discussion but it would be better to work towards a possible strategy rather than just telling the class what to do. You could show them a couple of squares of fabric and a container of water and ask them questions such as:

- How could we check to see if these fabrics are waterproof?
- What would we do with the water?
- How could we tell if the water is getting through the fabric?
- How could we catch the water if it goes through?
- How can we tell how much water gets through?
- How could we find out which fabrics are most waterproof?
- How can we test different fabrics and keep it fair?
- What equipment would we need to do this experiment?

At this stage, show the class how to test a piece of fabric using the method described in Group activities below (or ask for a child to help you demonstrate). This will help the groups when they start on the experiment themselves.

- **Results** – this is a record of what happened. On the activity sheets, guidance is provided and is graded for different abilities. For the preliminary demonstration you could show the class how to record one result using whichever method you feel best matches the average ability of the class or indicate briefly the different possible ways they might be asked to record their data.

- **Conclusion** – this is a statement or two to sum up what has been learned. There is a space provided on the activity sheet though it is important that the whole class discusses the groups' conclusions in the plenary session.

Group activities

Children should be clear about the aim of the experiment from the whole-class discussion and have some idea of how to carry it out and record their results. Read through Generic sheet 1. Children who can read this could have their own copies.

The method of testing described below is common to all the activity sheets and should be demonstrated at least once during the whole-class introduction:

1 Fix the fabric across the top of a container (such as a jamjar) using an elastic band. It is important that the fabric dips down into the jar to form a hollow.
2 Have some units of water prepared using a standard measure such as plastic bottle tops. It is best to have several ready since there may not be much time for refilling during the test itself. It is easier to fill these small measures by dipping them into a tub of water than by trying to pour in the correct amount to fill them.
3 Over a two-minute period, small measured units of water are added, one at a time, to the hollow in the fabric. Each measure of water should be added only when/if the previous one has drained away (the fabric can, of course, be wet but must not have a puddle). The group should count to see how many measures of water went through the fabric during the two-minute period and then record their results on their activity sheet.
4 The group should repeat steps 1, 2 and 3 for different fabrics.

Notes
- Measuring jugs or cylinders are not necessary with this method since it involves counting standard measures of water.
- Children who are capable of measuring volume could do so, though this can be fiddly as the volumes are small and would require many repeated measurements using appropriate equipment.
- The children are not asked to measure the amount of water that ends up in the jar, just how much they poured in. This avoids the problem that occurs with highly absorbent fabrics, such as thick cotton, which is far from waterproof but can hold a lot of water and, therefore, might give a deceptive reading if we recorded the amount of water in the container below.
- Fairness is an important factor – for example, each group should use the same measures of water each time, try to make the hollow in the fabric the same depth for each test and use the same size of container for each fabric it tests.

Activity sheet 1
This sheet is aimed at children who can do some parts of the experiment but require support in carrying it out, perhaps with fixing the fabric across the container and setting up measures of water. They will test three or four fabrics and record whether a fabric is waterproof or not by ticking a box (no numerical data). Before testing each one they should predict what will happen. To make a conclusion they fill in the name of a fabric that is waterproof and one that is not waterproof in the statement supplied. They then draw a picture of something that could be made from waterproof fabric.

Activity sheet 2
This sheet is aimed at children who can do the experiment themselves with little or no support. The children should test at least four fabrics and record the number of measures of water for each by shading tally boxes. Before testing each one they should predict what will happen. For the conclusion they are asked to fill in some words and draw a picture of something that could benefit from being made from waterproof fabric.

Activity sheet 3
This sheet is aimed at children who can do the experiment and record results themselves without support. They will record the number of measures of water by completing a table. Before testing each fabric they should predict what will happen. They should write a conclusion that comments on their results and, possibly, the experiment.

Plenary session
It would be appropriate to review briefly the ideas contained in aim, method and results before homing in and spending more time on the conclusion. As mentioned in the teachers' notes, conclusions sum up the results and hopefully answer the aim but can be much more than that. It is not

expected that all of these are tackled but conclusions can:

- go on to say how the information could be useful in real life
- mention ways of extending the experiment (for example, dripping water to simulate the effect of rain, using salty water or checking fabrics over a longer timescale)
- suggest ways of improving the method (to make it easier, more accurate, more informative)
- comment on something extra that was noticed or thoughts that were triggered by doing the experiment (such as, some fabrics get very heavy or stretch when wet).

This is a good opportunity to reinforce the fact that this is an investigation with an aim but is also an opportunity for observant thinkers to discover what might not have been expected or to go beyond the experiment itself. One of the exciting things about experiments is the unknown. The results might not match what had been expected but that is perfectly alright and is why we do experiments in the first place – to see what really happens. Every experiment has its limitations – it is not a failure if an experiment is seen to be in need of improvement.

It is good experimental practice to start off with a simple experiment and then refine and improve it to reach the standard or reliability required. It would actually be bad technique to begin with a complex setup. See the teachers' notes for factors such as surface tension that can affect results.

Ideas for support

Provide these children with a model of the equipment all set up so that they can copy the arrangement when setting up their own experiment.

Allow access to sample activity sheets with partially completed sets of results so that they can see how to fill in the information.

The children could have the experiment partly set up for them – for example, fixing the fabric across the container and setting up measures of water.

Display a whole-class conclusion where the ideas are added from the various groups for all children to refer to.

Ideas for extension

Ask these children to devise an experiment to find which wrapping material would be best for covering a parcel that has to go on a rough journey. Provide materials such as a wooden block, some sheets of sandpaper, a large tin or plastic jar, a variety of different papers for wrapping the wooden block and Generic sheet 1. Challenge them to come up with an aim and method for the experiment and if they come up with a reasonable proposal, let them try it out, record results and write a conclusion. Hint: a container can be lined with the sandpaper and the 'wrapped parcel' placed inside so that shaking or rolling the container causes wear and tear.

Linked ICT activities

Using 'Talking Write Away', 'Teaxtease', 'Clicker 4' or any other similar program that allows you to create wordbanks, set up a bank with words that can be used to complete sentences on the screen. Create a series of sentences with missing words for the children to complete. Show them how to insert the missing words using the word banks. Ask them to create a sentence of their own with a missing word to add to the sentences already prepared.

Materials put to the test

1 GENERIC SHEET

Use these steps to help you do your experiment.

The **aim** is what you are trying to find out. You can use just one sentence, such as 'My aim is to find out …'

The **method** is how you plan to do your experiment. The main parts are:

- deciding what to measure or record
- choosing what equipment to use
- deciding how to use the equipment and what to change
- making sure that you keep the experiment fair.

A diagram (picture) with labels can show what equipment you need and how to set it up. Then write a few sentences. Your sentences could be like these:

1. We will measure _____ using _____
2. The equipment we will use is shown in the diagram.
3. We will keep the experiment fair by keeping _____ and _____ the same during the experiment.

Results are what happened in your experiment. There are lots of ways to show what happened. Your teacher will help you to decide which is best. Results can be shown in one of these ways:

- a few words to say what happened
- a list of words put in order (for example, materials from hardest to softest)
- a table
- a graph or a chart
- a drawing or a photo.

The **conclusion** is a sentence or two to sum up what you found out.

58　CURRICULUM FOCUS • MATERIALS

PHOTOCOPIABLE

Name _____

Materials put to the test

ACTIVITY SHEET 1

Aim
Your task is to predict and then find out which fabrics are waterproof.

Method
- Pour a measure of water into the hollow and see if the water soaks through the fabric.
- If the first one soaks right through, add some more measures to see what happens.
- If any water soaks through the fabric it is not waterproof.

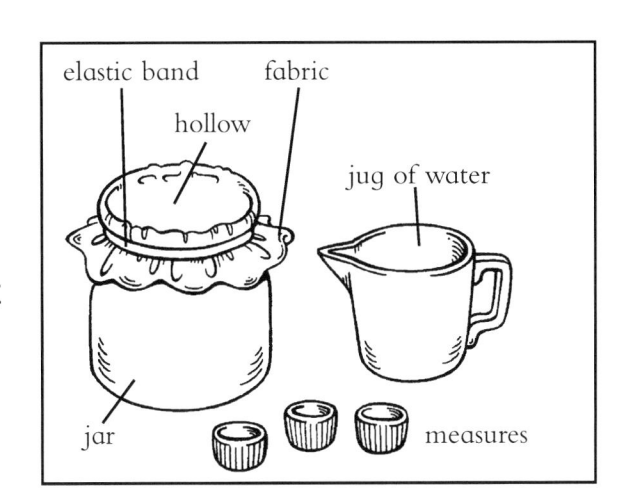

elastic band   fabric   hollow   jug of water   jar   measures

Results
Write down the name of the fabric and then tick (✓) one of the other boxes.

Name of fabric	Waterproof	Non-waterproof

Conclusion
Complete the sentence.

Some fabrics, such as _____ , are waterproof while others, such as _____, are not.

On the back of this sheet, draw a picture of something made from waterproof fabric.

PHOTOCOPIABLE

CURRICULUM FOCUS • MATERIALS   59

Name _____

Materials put to the test

ACTIVITY SHEET 2

Aim
Your task is to predict and then find out how waterproof different fabrics are.

Method
Pour a measure of water into the hollow and see if the water soaks through the fabric.
If the water soaks through, then add more but just one measure at a time. Count to see how many measures of water soak through in two minutes. Make a note of your results before testing another fabric.

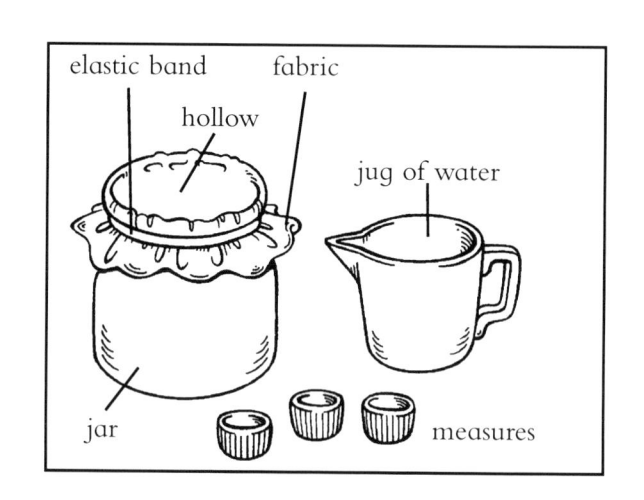

Results
Write down the name of the fabric and then shade in the boxes to show how much water went through.

Name of fabric	Shade in a box for every measure of water that soaks through

Conclusion
Complete the sentence.
Some fabrics, such as _____ , are more waterproof than others.
For example, _____ is more waterproof than _____ .

On the back of this sheet, draw a picture of something that could be made from waterproof fabric.

60 CURRICULUM FOCUS • MATERIALS

PHOTOCOPIABLE

Name _____

Materials put to the test

ACTIVITY SHEET 3

Aim
Your task is to predict and then find out how waterproof different fabrics are.

Method
Use this equipment to find out how waterproof different fabrics are.
Find out how many measures of water soak through in two minutes.
Think about how you can keep your tests fair.
Make a note of your results before testing another fabric.

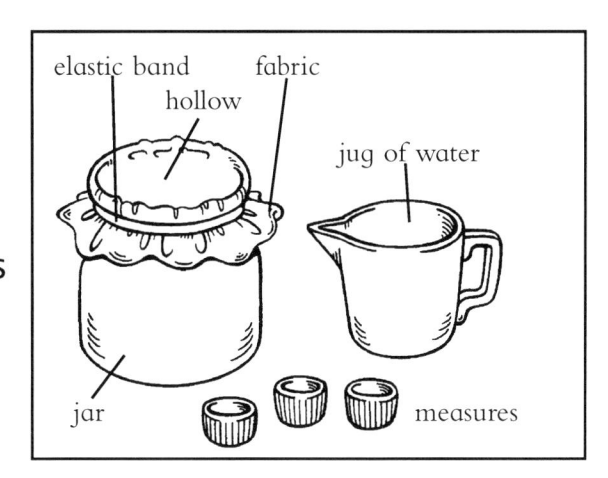

elastic band, fabric, hollow, jug of water, jar, measures

Results
Use the table to record the name of the fabric, how much water went through it and any other notes, such as whether the material changed in any way during the experiment – for example, did it get heavy, stretch or transparent?

Name of fabric	Number of measures soaked through	Notes

Conclusion
Sum up what you have found out by answering these questions.
- What did you find out?
- How could this information be useful?

On the back of this sheet write about how to improve this experiment or design a new experiment to test materials in other ways.

PHOTOCOPIABLE

CURRICULUM FOCUS • MATERIALS 61

6 Grouping materials

TEACHERS' NOTES

One way of grouping materials is to divide them up under the headings of solid, liquid and gas. Since by this stage the children have only dealt with solids this would not be useful. Another common way to group materials is into 'natural' and 'not natural' categories.

How do we know which is which?

There is no simple way of examining or testing a piece of material to tell whether or not it is natural. First identify the material and then use additional information to decide which group it belongs to. The simplest but least satisfying method would be to tell the children which materials are natural and which are not, perhaps by giving them a list of each. A more satisfactory way involves the children learning something of what we mean by 'natural' and about the sources of the materials. With this information and with some understanding, they should be able to choose, or at least agree with, natural and non-natural groupings. This is the approach taken in this chapter.

Natural or not natural

There are examples that belong obviously in one group or another, so start with these. The lists below give the more obvious examples. For some children, it may be better not to go beyond these.

Natural materials	Non-natural materials
wood	plastic
stone	paper
leather	glass
cotton	concrete
fur	brick
bone	fibreglass
sand	ceramics (fired clay)
straw	processed wood (for example chipboard, plywood)
clay (unbaked)	metal alloys (metal mixes such as brass, bronze, steel)
metals (pure, not alloys)	rubber (though some rubber is natural – see below)

So what counts as natural?
Natural is usually defined as 'occurring in nature'. The problem with this definition is that although every material we use comes originally from nature, most are changed, processed or combined to some extent to make them more suitable for our needs.

Early humans used natural materials with a minimum of processing – for example, a shelter might be a few long branches tied together with animal sinew and some animal hides thrown over the top. Today, wood from the same type of tree might be cut into logs, planed, treated with preservatives, laminated with plastic or cut into chips and then glued together to make chipboard. Wood counts as a natural material but, like any material, it can be put through many processes. This can be confusing for children – wood occurs naturally but chipboard does not.

Processing that doesn't count
Today most materials are processed in some way or other before use. If the materials start from a natural source and are then purified, extracted, cut to shape or just slightly adjusted to make them more suitable, they still count as natural. There are many such processes – polishing, spinning, tanning, filtering, purifying, grinding, rolling, drying and so on.

Metals are an example of a natural material that usually has to be extracted. Most metals are obtained by mining ore (the metal in its mineral state mixed in with other materials), which looks quite different from the pure metal. Extracting metal from its ore is an expensive industrial process. Pure metals count as natural because they are extracted from their ores – they are not being made. There are a few pure metals such as gold, silver and lead that do occur naturally and just need to be separated from the surrounding rock (or sand/gravel when panning for gold).

Synthetic or not natural

Non-natural materials are generally put together by combining and processing a number of materials.

62 CURRICULUM FOCUS • MATERIALS

Plastics are made from oil. The crude oil is heated and then chemical plasticisers are added, depending on the sort of plastic required. The two main types are thermoplastics (which can easily be softened and moulded) and thermosetting plastics (which do not soften on heating). Typical thermoplastic products are hard hats, pipes, bottles and toys. Typical thermosetting plastic products are found in cupboard door handles, saucepan handles, Formica work surfaces and so on. Plastics were developed throughout the twentieth century and have replaced natural materials for many uses.

Glass is synthetic and is usually a combination of silica (from sand), soda and lime. Glass was first made by the Egyptians over 3,000 years ago and was used for jewellery. Natural glass does occur but is not used commercially.

Concrete is a mixture of stones (aggregate), cement, sand and water. It is the most extensively used building material in the world and is thought to have been developed by the Romans. However, the process was then forgotten and it took another 1,300 years for concrete to be rediscovered.

Rubber can be either natural (from the sap of the rubber tree) or synthetic (produced from oil). This is a good example of how the 'natural' tag depends not on what the material is, but on how it was obtained. Most rubber produced today is synthetic and, like plastics, is made by adding chemicals to oil. The natural rubber that comes from the tropical rubber tree is obtained by draining sap from the tree and then separating out the rubber.

What to tell the children

It is easy for this all to get unduly complicated. The description above is given as useful background for the teacher. The activities in the lesson plan simplify these facts.

- Natural materials are already present on Earth and come out of the ground, from plants or from animals.

- Non-natural, synthetic materials have to be made, by mixing certain materials or chemicals. If it wasn't for people making them, the non-natural materials would not exist.

Plaster of Paris is a useful example covered in the lesson plan. It sets after being mixed with water and the chemical change that results produces a different material. Another example that could be used is PVA glue – it starts off as a white liquid but when left exposed to the air it turns into a clear solid. Emphasise to the children that when non-natural materials are made, they go through many changes in factories and processing plants. Normally people do not see these changes.

Other ways to group materials

There are, of course, many ways to group materials. In Chapter 4 they were grouped by their properties. The natural and non-natural materials divide into subgroups, which could lead to extension work:

- Wood is commonly classed as softwood or hardwood (this is to do with the tree species and not just the properties of the wood).

- Plastics are commonly grouped into thermoplastics or thermosetting plastics (see above).

Grouping materials

LESSON PLAN

Science objectives (Unit 2D)
- To know that there is a range of materials with different characteristics.
- To know that some materials occur naturally and some do not.
- To know the names of some naturally occurring materials.
- To know that some naturally occurring materials are treated (shaped, polished) before they are used.

Resources
- Some general sample materials, such as wood, sponge, stone, clear polythene and metal
- A specific example of a non-natural material – for example, plaster of Paris★ or modelling powder, and a plaster of Paris object (or similar material)
- Specific examples of a natural material in raw and processed state – for example, a branch or unshaped natural piece of wood, and an object made from wood (smoothed and shaped)
- moulds (optional)
- Generic sheet 1 (page 67)
- Activity sheets 1–3 (pages 68–70)
- Glue and scissors (or precut pictures from Generic sheet 1)

★There are other examples of non-natural materials that could be used here. But it is more interesting and clearer to choose an example that can be changed in the class to illustrate how much the material itself changes in the production of non-natural materials. This helps to contrast with the mere changing of shape, size or finish of natural materials that occurs in cutting and polishing.

Starting points: *whole class*

Show the class the sample materials (wood, sponge, stone, clear polythene, metal) and begin a discussion on the wide range of materials that exists. Take two materials at a time and hold them up to the class. Ask them to look at them and to say in what way they are different. Ask questions such as:

- Are these materials different?
- In what ways are they different? (Emphasise properties.)
- Are they the same in any way?
- This material must have come from somewhere. Where do you think it came from?

This last question might produce a correct response for something like wood or stone but it is likely that the children will not know what most original sources are.

Explain to the children that it is very useful to have all of these materials with all their different properties. Tell them that they are going to look at different objects and where their materials came from. Show them the object made from wood and ask the class where they think the materials came from. Show them the branch and point out that wood comes from trees.

Discuss with the class what would have been done to the wood from the tree to turn it into the object. Typical answers are:

- tree cut down;
- wood cut off the tree;
- bark removed;
- wood cut into planks or blocks;
- dried out;
- shaped by tools;
- sanded to smooth it;
- polished, varnished or painted.

Point out that, despite all the things that have happened, the wood inside the object is still pretty much the same as the wood in the branch (apart from being dried). If you cut into the branch and into the object they would look the same inside. Tell the children that this is called a natural material because we find and use it; we do not make it.

CURRICULUM FOCUS • MATERIALS

Show Generic sheet 1 to the children and talk through the three material stories. Cut out the pictures at the bottom of the page and, together, put them in the correct order.

Now show the class the powder and water that can be mixed to produce an ornament. Explain that plaster of Paris comes from a white rock which has been mined, ground to make a powder and then heated. Show the children the ornament. Discuss with them whether the ornament is the same as the powder and the water that were used to make it. If the children say that it is the same, then compare some of the properties of the powder and water with those of the ornament. It should be clear that the water and powder change when mixed and that you no longer have the same material afterwards. Tell the children that this is not a natural material because people produce plaster of Paris and mix it with water to produce a new material that is different from the original materials.

Ask the children to make an object from plaster of Paris (or an equivalent). Emphasise that there are separate stages in the process of making an object.

Group activities

Activity sheet 1
This is for children who would benefit from extra support. They are asked to sort pictures of objects into natural and not natural materials. They then have to cut up two sequences of material-changing processes and position the sequence pictures in the correct order. Remind them how this was done in the whole class activity.

Activity sheet 2
This is for children who need less support. They are asked to sort pictures of objects into natural and not natural materials. They are then asked to complete a sentence about each material-changing process shown.

Activity sheet 3
This is for more able children. They are asked to complete the sentences about the sequences of the material-changing processes shown. On the back of the sheet, they have to make a list of natural and not natural objects in the classroom.

Plenary session

Ask the children who completed Activity sheet 3 to say which objects in the classroom they think are made from natural materials. Do the other children agree? Discuss a few materials visible around the classroom. Where do they come from? What might have been done to them before arriving in the form that they are in now? Are they natural or non-natural? Ask the class if they know any local factories, craft workshops, mines or distributors who are involved in supplying or processing materials, or if anyone in their families is involved in such activities. Ask them about what life might be like on a desert island where our modern supplies of materials are not available.

Ideas for support

Produce a large table of the names of natural and non-natural materials.

Create a display of objects made from natural and non-natural materials.

Ideas for extension

Use a mould and some plaster of Paris to make a model. Craft shops often supply latex moulds of figures. Alternatively, use plastic trays (for example, from boxes of chocolates) as moulds or make a mould from soft modelling clay. Form a shallow trough, press a figure onto the inside bottom of the trough and remove it to leave an indentation in the clay then pour in the plaster of Paris.

Tell the children that wood can be either hardwood or softwood. Challenge them to find out which trees provide which type.

Research synthetic materials and find out what properties they have that are useful.

Linked ICT activities

Using a graphics program, such as 'Granada Colours', 'Fresco', 'Dazzle' or any other similar graphics program, tell the children that they are going to create a picture for a carrier bag for a shop that sells things made from a particular material, such as wood. Show them examples of different carrier bags and the pictures on them (taking care to use carrier bags that have holes in them for safety reasons).

Discuss what the children might draw to represent what the shop is selling. For example, if the shop sells items made from wood they could create images of trees. Show the children how to use the paintbrush tools and the fill tool and how to save and print the picture.

Grouping materials

1 GENERIC SHEET

Look at the stories of how materials are made. Decide for each whether it is natural or not natural.

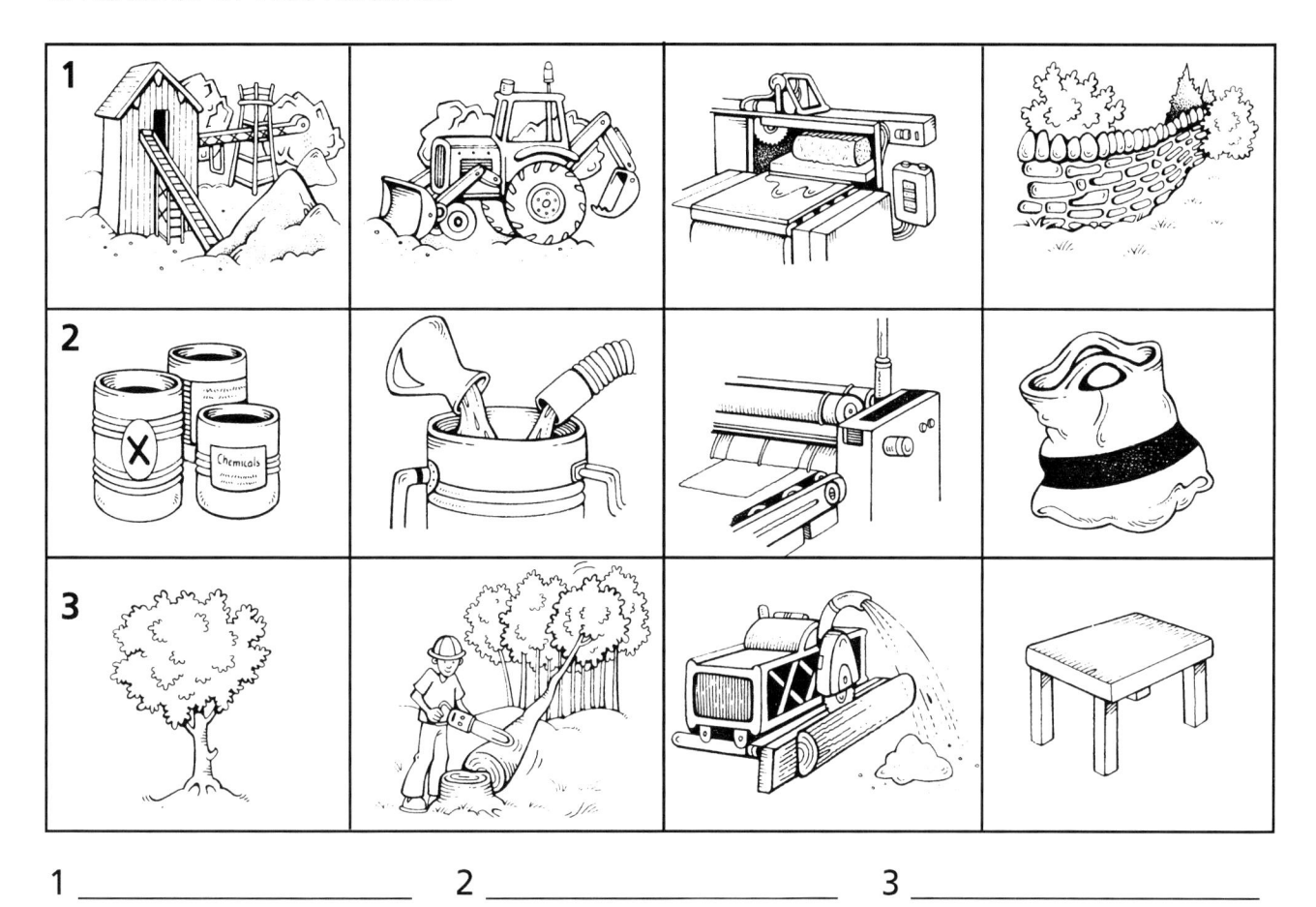

1 _____   2 _____   3 _____

Cut out the pictures below and stick them on a separate piece of paper in the correct order.

PHOTOCOPIABLE

Name _____

Grouping materials

ACTIVITY SHEET 1

Look at the objects below. Put a tick (✓) under the ones that are made from natural materials.

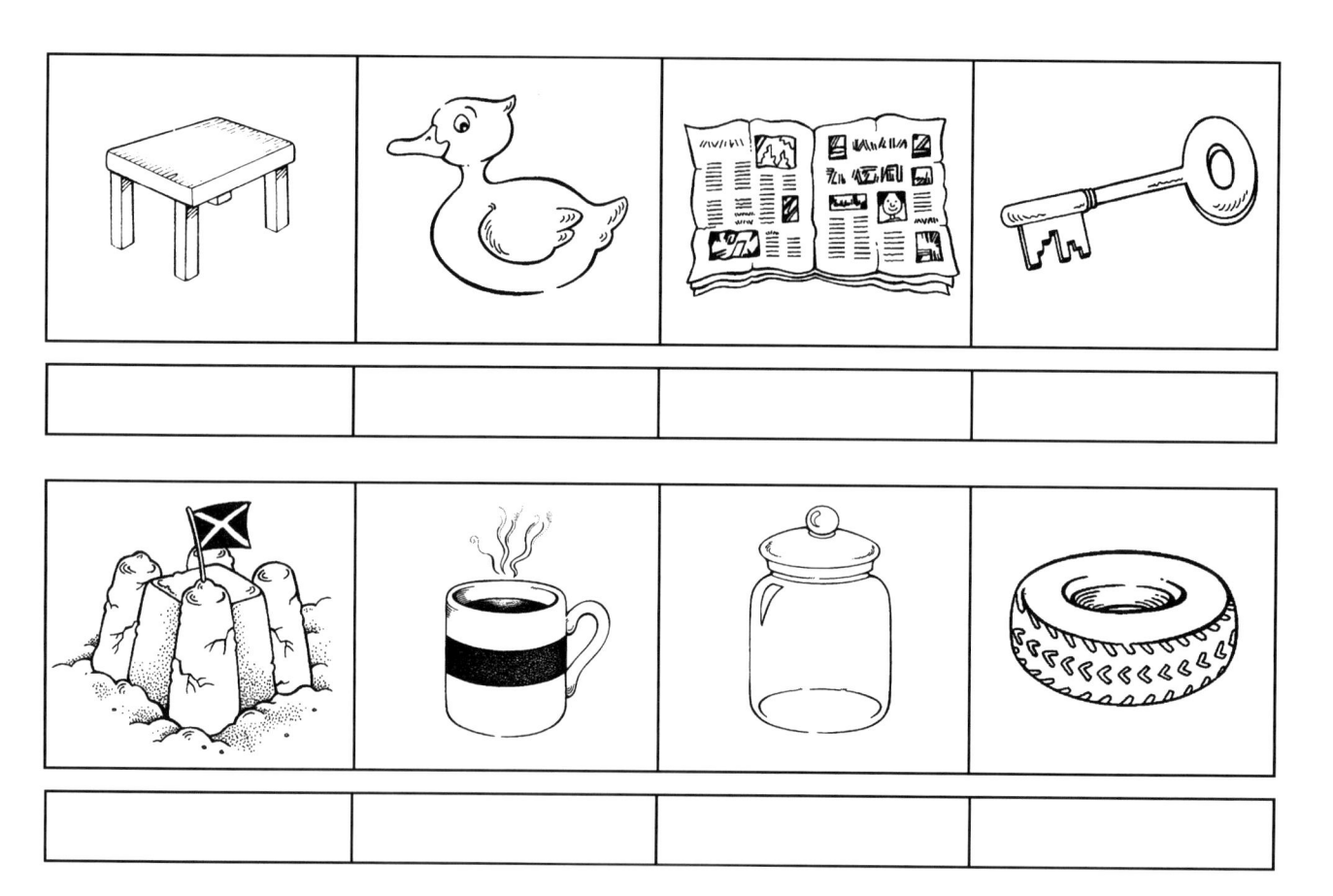

Cut the pictures below out and stick them on a separate sheet of paper in the correct order.

68 CURRICULUM FOCUS • MATERIALS

PHOTOCOPIABLE

Name _____

Grouping materials

ACTIVITY SHEET 2

Look at the objects and write 'natural' or 'not natural' under each one.

(pan)	(tyre)	(chair)	(belt)

(jar)	(sandcastle)	(newspaper)	(mug)

Complete the sentences.

a tree	tree cut down	cut into planks	made into table

To make a table, trees are _____, _____ and then _____ .

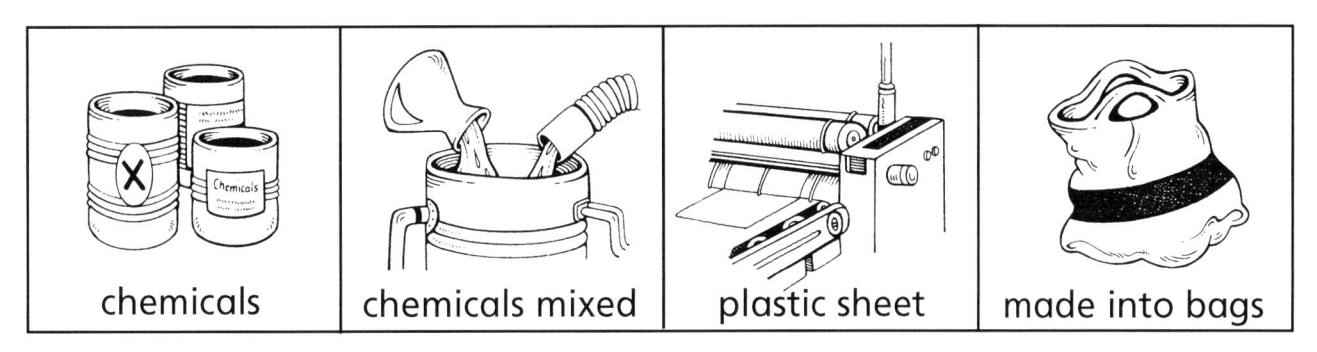

chemicals	chemicals mixed	plastic sheet	made into bags

To make a plastic bag, chemicals are _____ and made into a _____ which is then formed into bags.

PHOTOCOPIABLE

CURRICULUM FOCUS • MATERIALS 69

Name _____

Grouping materials

ACTIVITY SHEET 3

Complete the sentences.

To make a stone wall, stone is dug from a _____ and then _____ and made into a wall.

To make a plastic bag, chemicals are _____ and made into a _____ which is then formed into bags.

To make a table, trees are _____ and _____ and then made into a table.

WORD BANK
quarry   cut down   mixed   sawed   plastic sheet   cut into planks
---

Look around the classroom. On the back of this sheet, make a list of objects made from natural materials and a list of objects not made from natural materials.

Material workout

CHAPTER 7

TEACHERS' NOTES

Stretching, twisting, bending and squashing

These are all different ways of changing the shape of an object. Each of them involves applying forces. Although it is clear that the forces must be applied in different ways to investigate the desired change, children can easily become engaged in material wrestling bouts where it becomes difficult to see what type of force is being applied and what effect it is having. Structuring the practical work and breaking the experiment down into different areas of investigation can overcome these problems.

Keeping it fair

Children are very aware of the concept of fairness in everyday life but can often overlook or fail to recognise it in experiments. It is as well to explain fairness in terms of things with which they are familiar – for example, when running a race we have the same distance, the same starting time, the same age group, the same route and the same rules about types of footwear and forms of medication allowed. If we investigate something then, generally speaking, we aim to change only one thing at a time – in this case different materials. Ideally, everything else should be the same, but in reality this is difficult to achieve.

Fairness and forces

Perhaps the most difficult factor to keep constant is the size of the forces being used – it is natural to exert a small force and if nothing much happens to exert a bigger force until something does. This means that something that stretches easily is likely to be pulled with a small force and something that is more rigid will be pulled with a greater force. A device called a spring balance can be used to measure the size of the force exerted on an object – they are often simple devices consisting of a spring inside a casing, with a scale to show how much the spring has been stretched or compressed. The scales are marked in newtons, the units of force. To use a spring balance here would turn this into an overly complex experiment, but it may be worth a mention in discussing possible improvements to the experiment. It is sufficient to advise the children to try to use the same amount of force on each material they test, though we have to accept that considerable variation will occur.

Fairness and shape of material

Ideally, all of the sample materials should be of the same size and the same shape. Generally speaking, thin strands or sheets are more likely to bend and stretch easily than blocks of material. Shape, when taken to extremes, can make a huge difference so that glass, considered to be one of the most brittle of materials, can be flexible enough to roll into coils when in the form of a thin strand (glass optical fibres are used in communications systems).

It's best to try for rectangular slabs of material. Erasers could be used as samples of rubber. Materials like sticky tack, sponge and playdough can be acquired/cut/rolled into sheets of the same depth as the rubber and then sliced into blocks of a similar shape and size. Given the choice between not testing a material because you don't have a sample of the correct shape or size and testing a sample of a different shape and size, it would obviously be more informative to go ahead and test. Where such compromises are made, it is worth while pointing them out when discussing possible improvements to the experiment.

Types of material to use

A variety of materials such as glass, hard plastics and some metals are brittle and unsuitable from a safety viewpoint. Here the shape of the material is also an issue – thin strips of brittle material may snap and be a hazard whereas a block of the same material might be too strong to be snapped and, therefore, less of a hazard. It is best to limit the sample materials to those that are known to be safe even though the tests are not intended to test materials to destruction.

Materials that change when forces are applied should be tested but it would be a valid point to have at least one, such as a block of wood, metal or stone, that does not change visibly when tested. Too often children see no change results as an 'It didn't

CURRICULUM FOCUS • MATERIALS 71

work,' outcome. Do try to include some of these outcomes in experiments and emphasise the more positive view that proving that some materials don't change (stretch, bend and so on in this case) is just as valid as showing that some materials do. Indeed, it can be of great benefit – we wouldn't want wooden chairs and tables to change shape!

Suggested materials to use are:

- sticky tack;
- modelling clay/playdough;
- foam rubber;
- rubber (for example, erasers);
- expanded polystyrene as used in packaging;
- wooden block (for example, building brick or domino);
- plastic block (for example, building brick);
- clay.

Elastic and non-elastic

Many materials are capable of changing shape to a certain extent when forces are applied, but will return to their original shape when the forces are removed – these are described as elastic. Most children will be familiar with the fact that rubber is elastic and, indeed, the terms 'elastic band' and 'rubber band' are seen as equivalent. Other materials such as certain metals, plastics and wood are also elastic but not quite as obviously as rubber. The fact that strips of material made from plastic, metal or wood will spring back when bent a little and released is evidence of their elasticity. Their elasticity is easily overlooked due to the large size of the force required and, compared to rubber, the proportionately small amount that they stretch.

Most materials also have an elastic limit – they can be stretched up to a certain limit and will return to their original form, but when stretched beyond this limit will never return to their original shape. Thus a metal ruler will spring back if bent moderately but if forced beyond the elastic limit it will remain bent. Materials may snap eventually but can often go beyond the elastic limit and be deformed before reaching this breaking point. Children do not need to be informed of the elastic limit but should notice that some materials return to their original shape when the forces are removed (for example, foam rubber) while others do not (for example, playdough).

Applications of squashing, stretching, bending and twisting

People have deliberately used materials whose shape can be altered. Here are some examples.

- **Expanded polystyrene.** This is the same polystyrene used to make the brittle plastic cups used for cold drinks, but it has had air bubbled through it during manufacture. Expanded polystyrene is spongier and is used extensively in packaging and for plastic cups that hold hot drinks.

- **Crimped fibres.** The tiny strands used in clothing can be turned into twisted and springier versions of the original straight fibres. This makes clothing softer, stretchier and better at trapping heat.

- **Corrugated cardboard.** Cardboard is formed into ridges, often to make it stronger but also making it easier to squash.

- **Bungee jumping.** This involves using very stretchy ropes so that the people who jump are slowed down gradually and not hurt.

- **Nylon climbing ropes.** These have to be elastic. When climbers fall, the ropes can stretch to become 50 per cent longer. If they didn't, the sudden jerk of the rope could kill or hurt the climber.

- **Car crumple zones.** Cars are designed to crumple at the front and the back during crashes. This absorbs some of the impact so that people in the non-crumpling seating compartment are less likely to be hurt.

- **Cycle helmets.** They are made with expanded polystyrene as it can squash on impact to protect the wearer's head.

- **Guitar strings.** These strings are stretched to make them tighter and change the note. To play a note the guitarist stretches the string to one side and as it returns to its original position it creates a sound.

A simplified version of this type of information has been provided for children's use on Generic sheet 1 (page 76).

Material workout

LESSON PLAN 1

Science objectives (Unit 2D)
- To know that objects made from some materials can be altered by squashing, bending, twisting and stretching.
- To describe ways of making materials or objects change, using appropriate vocabulary.
- To explore materials using appropriate senses and making observations and simple comparisons.

Resources
- Samples of materials such as rubber, playdough, sponge, wood, clay and so on (see teachers' notes for related issues)
- Rulers
- Generic sheets 1 and 2 (pages 76 and 77)
- Activity sheets 1–3 (pages 78–80)

Starting points: *whole class*

Show the children a block of wood and a block of modelling clay. Try to make sure that they are the same size and that the block of modelling clay is smooth, regular and of an unfamiliar colour so that it is difficult for the children to be sure of what it is (this is preferable but not essential). Tell them your right/left hand is stronger than the other one. Gently pick up the modelling clay block in your stronger hand and the wooden block in the other hand. Close your hands and squeeze. Show the class what has happened. The children will, of course, guess that the different result is more to do with the material than the differing strength of your hands. Agree with them and suggest that you are going to do an experiment and that the aim of this experiment is to find out what happens to different materials when we try to stretch, squash and bend them.

Ask questions such as:

- What materials should we test?
- What materials do you think will change when we test them?
- How could we stretch them?
- How could we squash them?
- How could we bend them?
- How can we tell if they have changed when we do these things?
- How can we record the results?

Point out that the way we do the experiment is called the 'method'. There are lots of methods that could be used but to keep things fair they will all be asked to use the same method.

You may wish to point out the 'experiment steps' as listed on Generic sheet 1 of Chapter 5 (page 58). It is worth while trying to structure the experimental work in order to come to some clear conclusions about how different materials respond in these tests.

The activity sheets and Generic sheet 2 give the children directions on how to test the material for stretching, squashing and bending and how to record what happens. For more able children, there is the option of taking measurements though it is expected that these would have to be very approximate. An alternative for the more able would be to attempt to do identical tests on a selection of materials and then compare them.

Hand out copies of Generic sheet 2, which gives a statement of the aim and shows the method (the recommended ways of testing the materials). Read it through with the children. Show them the materials they will be testing and ask them to predict how each will do in the tests. This can be pretty general; a prediction for each material for each test is not required.

Ask for volunteers or select children to act as helpers. Demonstrate how to conduct one set of tests and how to record them on Activity sheet 1 (see Ideas for support [page 75] for possible techniques to use). Choose the playdough for the demonstration and emphasise that, when the children do these experiments, they should record the results for each test before moving on to the next. Tell them that they must use a fairly gentle force (one sufficient to stretch the material but not to rip it apart). You may decide to demonstrate how to record the results leaving them to repeat the experiment and record the results themselves, or you may ask the class to record their first set of results from the demonstrated experiment. The latter would be better suited to less confident children.

In the case of non-elastic materials such as playdough, the block will change shape after the first stage of the experiment. You should instruct the children as to whether they have to collect a replacement block of material for each of the three tests in the activity or whether they have to remodel it before moving on (this will depend on your resources and the ability of the class).

Tell the class that they have to get a set of results and make a conclusion; that is, they must complete the activity sheet for one material and return both the sheet and the material to you (they must not swap materials between themselves) before moving on to another material and another sheet (each child will need a new sheet per material tested).

Group activities

Issue one block of material and one activity sheet per child (see difficulty levels below). It is good practice to have a quick glance at the standard of the sheets as they are returned to you. This allows continuous monitoring of how the children are progressing and allows advice or additional support to be given before moving on. Children quickly recognise what is expected and are keen to come up to standard since it is a requirement for them to move on to testing another material. Without such monitoring it is possible for the children to create vast quantities of deformed materials but with little thought as to what it all meant.

Activity sheet 1
This sheet is aimed at children who can carry out simple tests, record what happened with a basic drawing, and draw a conclusion by ticking boxes. The children can go on to test more materials, perhaps using Activity sheet 2, if they have demonstrated sufficient experience in writing conclusions.

Activity sheet 2
This sheet is aimed at more able children who have the ability to write a conclusion by completing two sentences (perhaps with a little support) and who are capable of testing a good range of materials. They will need additional copies of Activity sheet 2 for each material, though there is the option of moving them on to Activity sheet 3 if they are deemed to be ready for a more challenging version of the experiment.

Activity sheet 3
This sheet is aimed at children who have the ability to carry out the experiment confidently, can draw a conclusion by writing a few sentences and can test a wide range of materials without difficulty. There is also the possibility of moving towards a more advanced experiment by taking measurements. This involves recording the width and the length of the block of material during the experiment. This can be tricky – it is not an easy measurement to make even for those who have good measuring skills and, of course, if tackled it could be limited to a few materials so that a comparison can be made. The advantage of taking measurements is that it reduces the dependency on opinion – it would be more relevant to take measurements for two materials that, to the naked eye, appear to behave in a similar way when tested. Although this extended experiment is supported on the activity sheet, it is included only as an option.

Plenary session

Remind the class of the parts of the experiment (see Generic sheet 1 from Chapter 5 on page 58) and that the aim of this experiment was to find out what happened if we stretched, squashed and bent certain materials. Point out that you had an agreed method (described on Generic sheet 2). On a display medium, such as a whiteboard or large sheet of paper, write the names of the materials as headings, each one with its own space.

Discuss the outcomes from the tests for the materials supplied and record some agreed descriptions of the results on the display medium – for example, stretched a lot, grew thinner, sprang back or stayed the same. Finally, discuss some of the children's conclusions. This is a good time to consider how the experiment could be improved and how the information acquired could be useful.

Ideas for support

To help with material types provide a visual display of the materials to be tested with prominent labels.

To help children who may have difficulty in drawing, provide cardboard templates so that children can draw the original shape of the block accurately – this can be useful for during and after results too as they can first draw the original shape in the space and then, using a different colour, add another line to show how it has changed. Alternatively, you can draw dotted line shapes in the results boxes of the master sheets before photocopying and distributing.

To help describe and compare the results, use Generic sheet 1 from Chapter 2 (page 22) and extend it to include appropriate terms such as 'long, longer, longest'.

Provide copies of Generic sheet 1 from Chapter 5 (page 58) to remind the children of the steps in an experiment.

Ideas for extension

Produce posters showing materials whose shape can be changed and add statements such as 'It is important that an elastic band can stretch because it can change its size to fit different things.'

Ask some of the more able children to design and carry out an experiment to test materials by twisting them. They should go through the experiment steps as described in Generic sheet 1 from Chapter 5 (page 58) and should only be given a range of materials to test when they have a clear aim, method and table to record results. Children are often keen to rush into the practical work – it is important that the necessary thinking and preparation are done beforehand. Having said that, sometimes children will need to do a little bit of trial and error work on a piece of material before deciding on the method. Make sure they are agreed on what they are doing and have discussed the expected outcome.

Linked ICT activities

Use a tape recorder for the children to record in groups the outcome of their experiments. Provide headings that they can work to; for example, 'What is my experiment about?' and 'What I did first.'

Each group should record the experiment as they go along. Encourage the children to keep listening to what they have recorded to allow them to sequence all their results.

The results of the experiments from each of the groups can then be played to the whole class. The recordings can be stopped at any point and the children asked to predict what they think will happen, they can then discuss whether or not their predictions were correct.

Material workout

Useful squashing, stretching, bending and twisting

Sometimes changing shape can be a good thing!

- **Bungee jumping.** People jump from high up using a special kind of stretchy rope. This slows down the people who jump so they don't get hurt.

- **Crumple zones.** Cars are made to crumple at the front and the back during crashes. When this happens, it helps prevent the people inside from getting hurt.

- **Cycle helmets.** These are made with a special type of foamy plastic. This squashes when it is hit hard. The plastic squashes to protect the head.

- **Guitar strings.** To make music the guitar string is pulled to one side and let go. The string stretches and springs from side to side to make a sound.

- **Skyscrapers.** These very high buildings can bend from side to side. When an earthquake shakes the ground the skyscrapers bend but don't break.

- **Elastic waistbands.** Lots of clothes have rubber bands in them. These can stretch so that they fit your body and spring back to grip on and to stay in place.

- **Measuring tapes.** A tape is made of material that bends easily so that it can be rolled up.

Material workout

Aim and method of testing materials

Aim
The aim is to see how pulling, squashing and bending change different materials.

- Use a medium amount of force in these tests.
- Try not to pull the material apart or destroy it.
- Try to keep one side of the material on the table when testing it.

Method
The materials are tested in these three ways:

Pulling

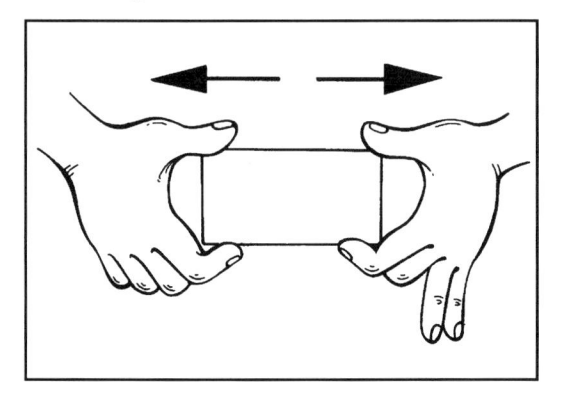

Squashing

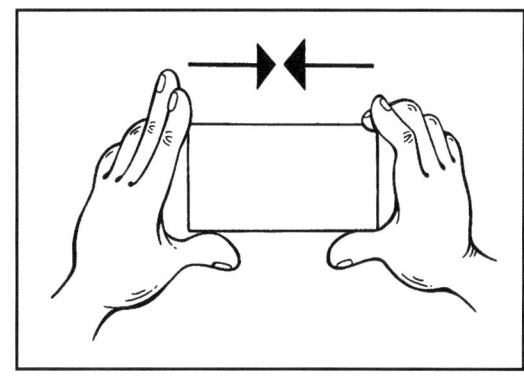

Bending

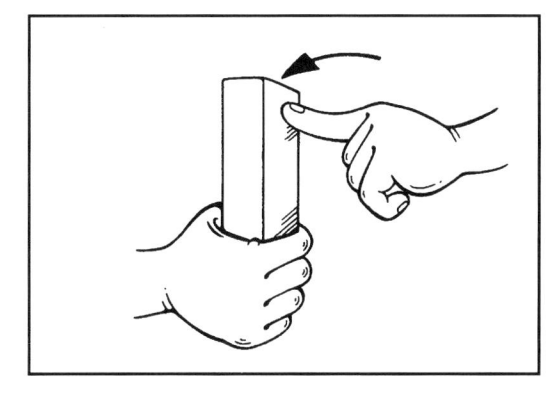

To keep the experiment fair, try to use the same size of force for each material you test.

Name _____

Material workout

1 ACTIVITY SHEET

Name of material _____

Results

Draw what the material looks like before, during and after the test.

Material being stretched – pull the material out at each end. ←□→		
Before	During	After

Material being squashed – push the material in at each end. →□←		
Before	During	After

Material being bent – hold the bottom then try to bend over. ↗□↘		
Before	During	After

Conclusion

The shape of this material changes during testing.   Yes ☐   No ☐

Name _____

Material workout

ACTIVITY SHEET 2

Name of material _____

Results

Draw pictures to show what the material was like before, during and after the test.

Material being stretched – pull the material out at each end. ←☐→		
Before	During	After

Material being squashed – push the material in at each end. →☐←		
Before	During	After

Material being bent – hold the bottom then try to bend over. ↗☐↘		
Before	During	After

Conclusion

The shape of the material:

during testing was _____

and after testing was _____

This material can be used for _____

_____

PHOTOCOPIABLE

Name _____

Material workout

3 ACTIVITY SHEET

Name of material _____

Results

Draw pictures to show what the material was like before, during and after the test. You could also measure the length and the width.

Material being stretched – pull the material out at each end. ←☐→		
Before	During	After
Length _____ Width _____	Length _____ Width _____	Length _____ Width _____

Material being squashed – push the material in at each end. →☐←		
Before	During	After
Length _____ Width _____	Length _____ Width _____	Length _____ Width _____

Material being bent – hold the bottom then try to bend over.		
Before	During	After
Length _____ Width _____	Length _____ Width _____	Length _____ Width _____

Conclusion

On the back of this sheet, write about what you noticed and how you could use this information.

Heating materials

TEACHERS' NOTES

General context

Heating materials is one of the oldest and most established ways of changing the materials in our environment. However, the heating process can have several different effects. Children will often presume that heat will melt an object or will burn it and, of course, this is sometimes true. It is good for children to attempt to predict outcomes, but it is important to be prepared for the fact that firmly held assumptions can sometimes be difficult to replace with fact. The children's limited experience may mean that they tend to be too quick to extend one specific result – for example, that chocolate melts when heated – to all solids. As explained below, there are many possible effects of heating materials. These effects can depend on the material, the temperature and the length of heating time as well as other less common factors. Children do not need a comprehensive knowledge of all of the possibilities but should be able to make observations of some changes caused by heat and describe a few examples of such changes.

Getting hotter

The simplest and most common effect of heat on a material is to make the material hotter. This may seem obvious but it is often overlooked in the pursuit of some more dramatic change. An electric kettle turns water at about 20°C to water at 100°C. The water is obviously at a higher temperature, though there are other subtler changes that occur along with this. Hot water becomes less dense so it tends to float above colder water. It also holds less oxygen dissolved in it – an important issue for marine animals.

In a similar vein, rubber can become much less flexible at very cold temperatures and become softer and more flexible at higher temperatures. Such comparatively minor changes in the properties of the materials are best overlooked at this level of study. These property changes with temperature tend to be gradual but, at specific temperatures, something more dramatic may occur. Steel (for example, in the form of a saucepan) can be heated on a gas ring with no obvious change except the rise in temperature. However, if the same material were to be heated to a temperature of about 1,500°C, it would suddenly undergo the more dramatic change of melting.

Melting

When solid materials are heated many of them will, when a high enough temperature is reached, melt – that is, turn to liquid. This occurs at a temperature known as the 'melting point'. When the same material is cooled, it will turn back to a solid – this occurs at a temperature known as the 'freezing point'. Generally, the melting point and the freezing point are the same temperature so that water, for example, freezes as it goes below 0°C and melts when it goes above 0°C.

Pure substances, such as water, melt at a very precise temperature whilst substances that are a mixture, such as chocolate, melt progressively over a range of temperatures, becoming soft and sticky at warm temperatures and a thin runny liquid at higher temperatures.

At higher temperatures, liquids turn to gas – this is called the 'boiling point' (100°C for water). When gases cool down, they turn back to a liquid or 'condense' at this same temperature. This change from solid to liquid to gas and back again can occur indefinitely. From the viewpoint of living things it is essential. The water cycle is one of the most important processes on our planet – water passes from oceans to clouds to rain and to rivers before returning to the oceans.

These changes between solid, liquid and gas are termed 'reversible'. Children do not need all of these ideas or the terminology, but they should learn that things melt and freeze and that the change can go both ways. In Chapter 10 they will look at changing water to steam.

Melting method

The children will be melting chocolate in the lesson plan (see pages 84–86). A tub of warm water with a lid on it can be used to melt chocolate. Place the chocolate on a piece of foil (this not only prevents the tub from getting covered in chocolate, but also allows the children to test the state of the chocolate by gently raising one edge of the foil a little without touching it). Place the chocolate and foil on top of the tub of warm water. The water should be fairly hot without being dangerously so. Chocolate will typically melt within about 15 minutes on top of a tub of medium hot water and will take around half that if hot tap water is used (60°C). Other factors that could affect the rate of melting are the thickness of the chocolate, the type of chocolate, the surrounding air temperature, the temperature of the chocolate before the experiment, the depth of water in the tub and the type of lid on the tub.

Equipment

There are various types of tub from which to choose. Margarine tubs and icecream tubs are not designed to withstand high temperatures and may buckle if subjected to very hot water. Tubs designed for holding hot foods or for microwave use are a better bet. Cooking foil or greaseproof paper should be cut so as to allow for the chocolate to spread out when melted. It would be advisable to do a trial run before letting the whole class do this.

Cooling

It is important that the children see that cooling reverses the process – this can be achieved quickly if the blobs of melted chocolate on the foil are carefully transferred to a freezer. Alternatively, the tubs could be used again but this time filled with ice cubes, with the advantage that the children can check on the process. More simply and more slowly the chocolate could simply be left to cool to room temperature.

Don't let the whole class touch the melted chocolate directly unless you are prepared for a major clean-up operation. Select a few volunteers instead.

Melting ice

The children will also be melting ice in the lesson plan (see pages 84–86). Supply groups with an ice cube on a tray or dish. Advise them not to touch the ice if it has come straight from the freezer (it may damage skin whilst still at its coldest). Allow them to observe and carefully touch it as it melts and to record any changes on their activity sheets. To show the reverse process allow them to fill various shapes or ice cube trays with water, place these in the freezer and return to them later.

Burning and chemical changes

When some materials are heated they may undergo other changes besides melting or getting hotter. These materials undergo a chemical change. This means that parts of the material react – that is, connect in different ways – and by so doing, make a new material.

Chemical changes are very common in the kitchen as part of many cooking processes. From boiling an egg and making toast to cooking a roast, chemical processes are going on. In these situations the food itself changes. It is not just hotter – when cooled the food is not as it was before.

Cooking a meal and heating a meal is not quite the same from the scientific view. Heating involves bringing the food up to a temperature for eating rather than changing the food itself by cooking (in convenience meals the cooking will normally have been already done in the manufacturing process).

Another chemical process, that of burning, is very familiar and, if the cook is competent, is not normally the same as cooking. In burning, a hot material reacts with oxygen in the air, sometimes producing even more heat as it does so. The new material (for example, ashes or burnt toast) is, of course, different because of this change. Burning generally occurs out of the kitchen. We call certain materials 'fuels' and burn them to generate heat – oil, gas, coal and wood are the most common examples. Less commonly we burn materials for light – candles and oil are examples.

Many materials, not just fuels, will burn if they are hot enough and are exposed to air. Even some unexpected ones, such as metals, will burn brightly in the right conditions. Flour, when finely powdered and swirled in the air can burn so fast that it is highly explosive.

We talk about burning electricity. However, this is not true burning – there is no change in the materials in the light bulb or in an electric heater, and there is no reaction with oxygen in the air. We do use up electrical energy, however, and back at the generating station where the electricity is made, coal, oil or gas may have been burned to produce that electricity.

It is not intended that children investigate burning in this chapter, but it is likely that some will ask about it or suggest burning as a possible outcome.

What to tell the children

Initially, the children should go ahead with the experimental work, hopefully acquiring evidence that will lead them to see that heating can cause different things to happen. When the results are being discussed, you can categorise the outcomes of heating things into three groups.

- Materials that just get hot (for example, metal).
- Materials that melt (for example, chocolate).
- Materials that change (for example, an egg).

It is not necessary to explain the detail of what is going on, but it is important that the children realise that:

- materials that change when heated remain changed even when they cool
- materials that melt to become liquid can be cooled again to become solid.

Ice and water

Safety note
Children should not touch ice that has just been taken out of a freezer since the extremely cold temperature can harm skin.

Most children will have some prior experience of melting ice, but there are always new things to be discovered. Here the emphasis is on using the senses, which in this case means sight and touch (see safety note). They should notice:

- the changing shape of the solid
- the appearance of liquid
- the change from the dry and straight-edged shape of ice fresh from the box to the wet dissolving rounded shape as it dissolves (once the melting point has been reached)
- the overall change from solid to liquid.

Children can touch the ice after it has been out of the fridge long enough to have warmed up from the possibly harmful temperatures of the freezer itself. At first, there may seem to be little change whilst the ice initially heats up from, say, −30°C towards 0°C, but once the surface of the ice reaches 0°C the obvious change of it starting to melt will occur.

Heat … What heat?

Because of the low temperatures involved, some children may not realise that we are heating the ice. Whenever something is colder than its surroundings it takes in heat and when anything is hotter than its surroundings it gives out heat. Point out that the ice is soaking up heat from the air around it and by so doing it makes the room a little cooler.

Some examples of reversible changes

In reversible changes the melting caused by heating can, of course, be reversed by cooling. Some of these occur naturally – for example, lava – whilst others are used in manufacturing – for example, plastics and metals.

Here are some examples:

- ice to water
- solid chocolate to liquid chocolate
- solid wax to liquid wax (candle making)
- solid metal to molten metal (poured into moulds and cooled to make desired shape)
- rock to lava (lava emitted by volcanoes forms volcanic rocks such as basalt)
- plastic to molten plastic (some plastics are heated and moulded but not all)

Some examples of irreversible changes

Irreversible changes caused by heating are a result of changes in the structure of the material (links between atoms are altered). Cooling reduces the temperature but doesn't reverse the changes in the chemical structure, so we cannot unboil an egg! Some changes are used deliberately, as in cooking, whilst others happen naturally or accidentally.

Here are some examples:

- cake mix to baked cake
- bread to toast
- fresh egg to boiled egg
- solid butter to melted butter (this does change, not dramatic, remains clearer)
- raw potato to cooked potato
- raw meat to cooked meat
- wood to ashes
- clay to ceramics.

Heating materials

Science objectives (Unit 2D)
- To know that materials often change when they are heated.
- To know that many materials change when they are cooled.
- To suggest how some materials might change when they are cooled.
- To make observations and simple comparisons.
- To construct a table to record observations.
- To explore melting ice using appropriate senses.

Resources

- Materials for keeping areas clean and maintaining hygiene
- A supply of hot water
- Plastic tubs with flat lids to be used as hot areas
- A bar of chocolate
- Materials/items for demonstrating the effects of heating, such as bread, an egg, butter and means for cooking egg and toasting bread (cake mix and the means to bake the cake are another option)
- Materials/items for children's experiments on effects of heating: ice cubes, chocolate squares, clay (clay is optional – it also requires teacher access to means of baking clay)
- Metal samples (such as coins)
- Generic sheets 1 and 2 (pages 87 and 88)
- Activity sheets 1–3 (pages 89–91)

Safety note
Children should not be allowed access to very hot materials or get close to dangerous equipment. If such materials and equipment are used then appropriate precautions should be taken and heating demonstrated at a safe distance or under safe conditions.

Where any form of food preparation is to be done, hygiene must be scrupulously observed. This includes washing hands, using clean utensils and disinfecting surfaces. Pay heed to the latest advice or regulations.

Starting points: *whole class*

People change materials by various processes. Remind the children that they learned this when studying natural and non-natural materials.

The introduction to the lesson should ideally involve some practical examples of materials being changed by heat. What is possible will depend very much on the resources available. None are technical or scientific, but some depend on using kitchen equipment.

If it is not possible to demonstrate the whole process within the class then there are other options.

- Show previously prepared/acquired 'before and after' examples.

- Show the sample before heating, take it away, heat/cook it and then show the class the result, perhaps the next day.

Of course, it would be preferable for the class to see the whole process.

One easy way of creating interest and introducing the topic is to show the children a wrapped bar of chocolate that has been previously warmed, bent and then cooled to give it an unusual shape. You can ask them how it came to be bent like this and demonstrate that it is rigid and cannot easily be changed by forcing it without it being broken. (This ties in with the previous work on stretching, bending and so on in Chapter 7.)

Now that you have established that heat can change things, carry out the following demonstration to show that heat doesn't always cause noticeable changes. Show the children two identical cups, each with the same level of water and an identical metal teaspoon in it. Don't reveal to them that the water in one cup is warm while in the other it is cold. Ask them if they can see any difference in the two set-ups. Tell them that there is an important difference and challenge them to guess what it might be (you may wish to remind them of the use of different senses covered in Chapter 1). Discuss the fact that sometimes heat causes no effect other than to make the material warmer. Let someone come out and feel each spoon and tell the others what they have found out.

Tell the children that they are going to investigate the effect heat has on things. Ask them questions such as:

- What does heat do to materials?
- What materials do you heat at home?
- Why do we heat materials up?
- What devices in the house are designed for heating things?
- Would it matter if we couldn't heat up things?
- Are there things that change when they are heated up?
- Are there things that don't change when they are heated up?

Melting of chocolate and ice will be done later as group experiments. Choose from the demonstrations listed below according to your resources.

- Tell the class you are thinking about starting a school breakfast service and reveal to them some bread, some butter and an egg. Ask the class if any of them like to eat raw eggs. Ask them why not. You may wish to show them a raw egg in a clear container so that they can more readily describe its properties. Tell them that, in fact, they should not eat raw eggs because of the danger of salmonella. Cook the bread, butter and egg and show the children the results (or show before and after examples). Discuss the changes as a whole class, using Generic sheet 1. Note that butter not only melts when heated but changes to become clearer when it cools.

- Involve the children in making a cake. Keep a little of the original mixed ingredients to compare with the finished cake. The children can help mix but appropriate hygiene precautions must be taken. Cook the cake (no direct child involvement due to safety issues) or make arrangements for this to be done. Discuss the differences between the original mix and the baked cake.

- Give the children some clay to make into models/shapes. Keep back some of the clay. Bake the shapes (or arrange for the clay to be fired) and then compare before and after. If you have access to a method of baking the clay, then this is a good activity, firstly because it shows a soft material becoming hard due to heat and secondly because it is not reversible. Children should be kept away from the oven/kiln and from the baked clay until it has cooled.

Group activities

The groups should go on to investigate the effect of heat on chocolate, ice and butter, and for more advanced children, bread and egg (supervised).

Melting chocolate can be great fun, especially if you let the children eat it after it has cooled. The basic idea is to place a square of chocolate on a piece of foil and then to warm it gently. It can then be observed melting. Afterwards, by putting it in a cool location, it can be seen to solidify again. One method of melting chocolate is described in the teachers' notes (see pages 81 and 82) though you could use other methods or adapt this one to suit your resources.

Activity sheet 1
This is for children who can make basic observations of two materials, complete a chart to show what happens and, with assistance from a word bank, complete a conclusion.

Activity sheet 2
This sheet is aimed at children who can make observations of three materials, complete a chart to show what happens and record their results with assistance from a word bank.

Activity sheet 3
This sheet is aimed at more able children. They have to make observations of four materials and complete a chart to record their results. They then go on to do another experiment comparing ice, chocolate and metal. They use exactly the same process as for chocolate, but place all three samples at the same warm and cold locations at the same time.

Plenary session

Draw out by discussion the different ways in which the materials were affected by heat and talk about some examples of each. Emphasise that there are three different outcomes that have been met in their tests:

1. Material may just get hot (for example, metal).
2. Material may melt (for example, chocolate, ice).
3. Material can be changed (for example, an egg, cake, toast, clay).

Chat with the class about what happens when these materials are then cooled. Do they return to what they were before or do they stay changed permanently? You may wish to choose some children to try some of the extension work that involves comparing cool and warm samples of the same material.

Ideas for support

Set up an example of the chocolate melting equipment arranged exactly as you want the groups to do it. Leave it visible for groups to copy until they have set up their own.

Produce a large display of the three different outcomes discussed in the plenary session and add examples of each in pictures or words.

Ideas for extension

Compare the properties of some materials, such as modelling clay, playdough, sticky tack, rubber and clay, in cold and warm conditions. Take two samples of each, one warm and one cooled, and compare them by testing, as in Chapter 7 (bending, stretching, squeezing). Generic sheet 2 may be useful for this exercise.

Do a comparative study of melting using three different types of chocolate (for example, white, milk and plain).

List all of the possible devices that are used to heat foods in a kitchen and describe how the heat affects the substance that it heats.

Linked ICT activities

The children should be aware of everyday items that use information technology and have an understanding of how they are used in the world around them.

Talk to them about objects they use or objects they know about that will heat things up or cool things down. Use old catalogues for the children to cut up and find pictures of such objects, such as a hairdryer, fan and fridge. Talk to them about how they think the objects work; for example, do they press a button, press a switch and so on.

Use the pictures to make a collage of objects that make things hot and those which will make things cold.

If you have a digital camera available take some images of household objects that the children will recognise.

Heating materials

Examples of how to complete this sheet using words only.

Material	What the materials were like...		
	Before heating	When heated	Cooled down
clay	dark, soft, flexible, shiny	lighter coloured, hard, stiff, brittle	lighter coloured, hard, stiff, brittle
cake	runny, yellow, shiny, very soft	firm, brown, dull	firm, brown, dull

It can be better to use words and pictures.

Material	What the materials were like...		
	Before heating	When heated	Cooled down
clay	dark, soft, flexible, shiny	lighter coloured, hard, stiff, brittle	lighter coloured, hard, stiff, brittle
cake	runny, yellow, shiny, very soft	firm, brown, dull	firm, brown, dull

Heating materials

Examples of things that might be affected by cooling or heating

Predict what they will be like when cool and when hot, for example in a freezer and in hot sunshine. If possible, try these out to see if you are right.

Rubber gloves	Honey	Modelling clay
When hot _____	When hot _____	When hot _____
When cold _____	When cold _____	When cold _____

Wooden ruler	Plastic plate	Wax candle
When hot _____	When hot _____	When hot _____
When cold _____	When cold _____	When cold _____

Name _____

Heating materials

Activity Sheet 1

Aim To find out what happens when materials are heated.

Method Heat a square of chocolate and then cool it down. Watch an ice cube melt and then freeze some water to make ice.

Results Write or draw what happened.

Material	What the materials were like...		
	Before heating	When heated	Cooled down
chocolate	hard, square shape, stiff		
ice	hard, cube-shape, clear/white, dry		

Conclusion

When we heat materials, sometimes they m _ _ _ like ice does and sometimes they c _ _ _ _ _ like an egg does.

WORD BANK

hot cold hard soft melt freeze change square cube rounded
blob flat pool solid liquid dry sticky runny jelly wet clear
white brown stiff bendy

PHOTOCOPIABLE

CURRICULUM FOCUS • MATERIALS 89

Name _____

Heating materials

2 ACTIVITY SHEET

Aim To find out what happens when materials are heated.

Method Heat a square of chocolate and then cool it down. Watch an ice cube melt and then freeze some water to make ice. Heat a large knob of butter and then cool it down.

Results Fill in the table below. Use pictures, your own words or words from the word bank at the bottom of this sheet.

	What the materials were like...		
Material	Before heating	When heated	Cooled down
chocolate	hard, square shape, stiff		
ice	hard, cube-shape, clear/white, dry		
butter			

Conclusion

When we heat materials, sometimes they _____ like ice does.
Sometimes they _____ like an egg does.

WORD BANK
hard soft melt change freeze square cube rounded blob flat pool
solid liquid dry sticky runny jelly wet clear white brown stiff bendy

---

90   CURRICULUM FOCUS • MATERIALS   PHOTOCOPIABLE

Name _____

Heating materials

3 ACTIVITY SHEET

Aim To find out what happens when materials are heated.

Method Heat a square of chocolate and then cool it down. Watch an ice cube melt and then freeze some water to make ice. Heat a slice of bread and an egg and then cool them down.

Results Fill in the table below. Use pictures or words.

Material	What the materials were like…		
	Before heating	When heated	Cooled down
chocolate			
ice			
bread			
egg			

Extra experiment
Compare heating metal, ice and chocolate. Heat them in exactly the same way and for the same length of time. Make a table to record your results.

Conclusion
When we heat materials, sometimes they _____ like ice does, sometimes they just get _____ like metal does and sometimes they _____ like an egg does.

PHOTOCOPIABLE

CHAPTER 9

Water world

TEACHERS' NOTES

General context

Water is the most important and the most common liquid on the planet. Children tend to think of water in the familiar liquid form that we most commonly encounter. From previous work and perhaps their own experience, they should know that water can exist in the form of ice (a solid), but may not be accustomed to thinking of it as steam (a gas).

At the temperatures experienced on our planet, most materials are either solid or gas – water and oil are two common exceptions. In extremely cold circumstances, such as on the planet Pluto, almost everything is solid, even materials that would be gases on Earth. On the other hand, if an Earth-like planet were to orbit much nearer to the Sun, steam would be the norm rather than water, and materials that we think of as solids – for example, the metal lead – might be in liquid form.

We tend to be limited in our vision by our own experience. We see the materials on our planet through a 'temperature window' of about −20°C to +30°C. In different circumstances it could all look very different.

Vocabulary

It is not necessary to use scientific terminology at this level, although it can sometimes be difficult to avoid doing so when trying to discuss the topic in depth or with clarity. Some vocabulary is essential and much of it will already be familiar to the children. Other vocabulary, not essential but useful, is listed for reference.

Essential vocabulary	Useful vocabulary
heating	solid
cooling	liquid
boiling	gas
freezing	condensing/
melting	condensation
ice	evaporating
water	water vapour
steam	state

Experimental steps

The children have met the necessary steps in an experiment in at least two earlier experiments, yet it is again relevant to raise their awareness of the experimental steps – aim (including prediction), method, results and conclusion (see Generic sheet 1 of Chapter 5 on page 58). These steps do not need to be covered with great rigour and it would not be expected that the children should memorise them. Their use at these early stages should help the children become familiar with the scientific process and help provide a structure to their experimental work. There has to be a balance between children's natural tendency to wander randomly as their minds and inclinations take them and staying on target in order to get some results.

Fair experiments

When considering the method to use, fairness should always be an issue. This particular experiment is one that lends itself well to this issue. The lesson plan involves the teacher deliberately suggesting an unfair experiment. This is a valuable learning opportunity where children can spot and remove unfairness, something not possible if they are given a method in which unfairness has already been eliminated.

Extending experiments

Ideas and creativity are valuable. The fact that the children's inquisitive minds lead them to ask questions not encompassed in the experiment's original aim should never be a reason for not following them up. Rather, such suggestions should be seen as things of value, mentioned in the conclusion and, if time, resources and safety allow, be the aim of the next experiment. The aim and method of every experiment should be considered and agreed, results should be recorded and a conclusion should be discussed (also see safety issues below).

Science as an adventure

Sometimes the most worthwhile and exciting experiments are those which have a 'What if…?' spontaneity about them. Science is about discovery and tends to lose its zest if it gets stuck in the groove of just doing the worksheet and checking what you already know. This more open-ended type of experimental work is not covered by any worksheet because it cannot be. It comes from some unpredictable spark of imagination in the human mind and, even though the teacher may not know the outcome, it should be encouraged, at least discussed and preferably followed up and tried. Children can sense when they are moving onto untrodden ground and will often respond with a higher level of enthusiasm and involvement.

Safety notes

Children should not touch ice that has just been taken out of a freezer since the extremely cold temperature can harm skin.

Do not allow children to go ahead and carry out new experiments without consulting you. They may well suggest a minor variation that will cause no additional hazards. If their suggestion is substantially different then there is a possibility that the new set-up could involve a danger to themselves, to others or to the equipment/surroundings – it would be wise to consider whether it is suitable and to carefully monitor it if it does go ahead. Sometimes such suggestions are better carried out as a demonstration experiment where you can be directly involved and the children who made the suggestion can be the assistants.

Heat … from the air and the melting ice experiment

In Chapter 8 it was mentioned that the children might not realise that the ice was being heated by its surroundings. In this activity they move on to investigate how quickly heat is being absorbed from the surroundings by measuring how quickly ice melts. The temperature of the air is the obvious factor but there are others that will affect the rate of melting.

- Heat radiated from warm objects such as heaters, lights or the Sun.
- Air movement. If the air is moving rather than still it will tend to melt the ice more quickly.

If the melting rate of the ice cubes is to be used to estimate the temperature of different parts of the room, then there are other factors to keep constant.

- The size of the block of ice.
- The starting temperature of the ice.
- The shape of the ice.
- The way in which the ice is held.

In order to see a difference in the results, it would be best to include in the test some significantly warmer and cooler areas.

Water world

LESSON PLAN

> **Science objectives (Unit 2D)**
> - To use their knowledge about what makes ice melt to plan what to do.
> - To recognise what would make a test unfair.
> - To use results to draw a conclusion about which place is warmest.
> - To use a table to make a record of observations.

Resources

- Trays of ice cubes with loops (see group activities)
- A set of identical plastic cups
- Six blocks of ice of different shapes and sizes (made using plastic bags)
- Clear containers (for example, jam jars) or clear plastic cups
- Six different containers – for example, clear plastic bag, jamjar, tin, ceramic cup, plastic and cardboard boxes
- A clock or timer
- Activity sheets 1–3 (pages 97–99)

Starting points: *whole class*

This chapter is about melting ice and is a group activity. Tell the class that they are going to investigate ice melting. Ask questions such as:

- What makes ice melt?
- Are there any places in the room where ice might melt quickly?
- If we put two pieces of ice in different parts of the room and one melted more quickly, what would that tell us?
- How could we measure how quickly they melted?
- How would you know that the ice had melted?

Tell the class that seeing how quickly ice melts might be a good way to find the warmest place in the room. Show the children the selection of different shaped and sized blocks of ice and suggest that you use these. Show them the clear plastic bag, a jamjar, a tin, ceramic cup, plastic box and a small cardboard box and suggest that you use these to hold the blocks of ice. Ask them if that would be alright. Ask them if finding out which of the ice blocks in these containers melted first would be a fair way to find the warmest place in the room.

Discuss what you would need to do to make it a fair experiment (shape of ice, size of ice, type of container). Ask them to predict what might happen. The section in the teachers' notes called 'Heat ... from the air and the melting ice experiment' covers issues relevant to this experiment.

Group activities

Preparation

You will need to have some trays of identical ice cubes with loops. The loops can be made from a variety of materials. To keep the experiment fair the loops should all be placed into the trays of water and become embedded in the ice in the same way. It is better if some of the loop is inside the ice rather than just around its outer edge, hence the wire loops are shown curled up at the ends. Floppy material like string can be awkward to position.

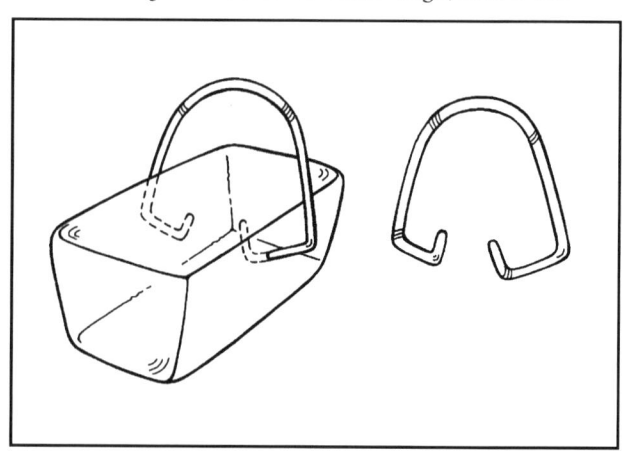

Suggested items to form a loop:

- Plastic-coated twist wire (as used for sealing bags or for gardening purposes) can be shaped like a figure D with the flat edge resting on the bottom of the tray. (This wire is obtainable from shops that stock freezer bags or gardening suppliers who may call it 'twist twine'.)

- Small rubber bands (for example, 3cm diameter) work well if they can be reliably positioned in the trays (heavy-duty bands are less floppy).
- Paper-clips can be bent in the middle to form the letter 'T'. Invert the T shape, placing the shortest side into the tray, leaving the longest loop of the clip rising out of the water/ice.
- Strips of plastic or cardboard in figure 'D' shapes could be used, but have been found to be a bit unreliable as they tend to just stick to the surface of the cube instead of embedding.

Once the loops are in the trays, fill them as closely as possible to the same depth. Once frozen it is best to release the cubes using a little warm water on the bottom of the trays to avoid cracking them. The extracted cubes can be stored in the freezer in a bag so that the same tray can be used to make additional cubes. It is, of course, important to use the same type of tray for all of the ice cubes.

Discuss and allocate places in or near the classroom where the temperature is going to be checked. In order to see some difference in the results, it would be best to include in the test some significantly warmer and cooler areas. Normally there is very little difference in the air temperature around a room. Cool possibilities are outside the window, outside the door or in a fridge (not a freezer or else the ice would never melt). Warm possibilities are near radiators or heat sources, on top of a fridge, near a strong light source and in sunshine. Care should be taken that water cannot reach mains electricity. Some average temperature locations should also be included.

Show the class a couple of identical ice cubes and show them how they can be suspended over a tub by putting a pencil/stick through the loop and hanging the cube across the open top of a tub. Tell them that these will be put in the different places and that they will measure how long it takes for the ice to drop off the loop. Issue sheets and equipment, ask them to place the cubes in the allocated places at the same time and then start the clock. One advantage of the cube on a loop is that the ice falling off the loop can be used to define a specific moment when the time is to be measured. In a quiet room, or if someone is close and listening, the cube can be heard dropping into the tub. You may wish to allocate listeners/watchers at each of the areas. Alternatively, you could set up a check system where children check the cubes every 15 minutes or so, though if several cubes drop within one time interval the order in which they drop cannot be told.

The cubes could take from 15 minutes to several hours to fall depending on the temperature of the location. You could move the class on to some alternative work while you wait for the results – for example, you could move on to the steam demonstration experiment in Chapter 10.

Activity sheet 1

This is for children who can make basic observations and can record in a simple manner. They complete the table of observations by ticking boxes and complete statements to make a conclusion. The teacher could write in the place names before photocopying the sheet.

Activity sheet 2

This is for children who are more confident with observations and they use their table more as a record of time than as a check sheet. They are expected to more fully analyse their results and to complete sentences.

Activity sheet 3

This sheet is aimed at more able children who can make observations, complete a table and then work out the overall time. They have to draw a conclusion without aids or prompts.

Plenary session

Discuss the experiment outcomes and anything discovered or that has arisen about:

- melting
- warm and cold places as measured by the experiment
- ways of measuring heat
- keeping things fair.

Ideas for support

A large chart could be produced with the words (and possibly pictures) depicting ice, water and steam with arrows labelled 'heat' and 'cool' linking the words to indicate the processes that cause the changes.

A vocabulary list of relevant terms could be posted in a prominent place or issued as a handout (see teacher's notes for words to include in a list).

Ideas for extension

The class could do a weather survey noting the number of days that are cloudy, sunny, dry and rainy. Alternatively, the class could do a cloud survey, estimating and taking a note of what percentage or fraction of the sky is covered with clouds at different points during the day or week.

The children could write a story or draw a picture of what it would be like if there were too little or too much water, or if the water had all frozen.

Linked ICT activities

Using a data sorting program, pick a picture. Work with the children on a daily basis to record what the weather is like on each day over a period of two to three weeks. When all the data has been collected discuss the results with the children. Find out how many days it rained, how many days there was sunshine, if it snowed on any of the days and so on.

Alternatively record the weather over a period of a week using the program 'My World 2' and the file called 'Chart'. This file will allow you to create a block graph for the children by dragging weather symbols onto the graph. This can be saved and the results discussed with the children. This could be a whole class activity if you have a projector and a whiteboard.

Name _____

Water world

ACTIVITY SHEET 1

Aim
To predict and then find out if ice melts more quickly in a warm place than in a cool place.

Method
Place cubes of ice in different places and see which melt first.

Results
Each time the cubes are checked record the results in the boxes.

Place	Put a ✓ if the ice is still there, a ✗ if it has gone

Conclusion
Ice melts faster in _____ places.

The warmest place is _____

The second warmest place is _____

PHOTOCOPIABLE

CURRICULUM FOCUS • MATERIALS 97

Name _____

Water world

ACTIVITY SHEET 2

Aim
To predict and then find out if ice melts more quickly in a warm place than a cool place.

Method
Place cubes of ice in different places and see which melt first.

Results
Shade in the boxes until the ice cube has melted.

Place	Time to melt (every box represents __ minutes)

Conclusion
Ice melts faster in _____ places and more slowly in _____ places.

Start with the warmest. The five warmest places in order are:

_____ _____ _____

_____ _____

98   CURRICULUM FOCUS • MATERIALS   PHOTOCOPIABLE

Name _____

Water world

3 ACTIVITY SHEET

Aim
To predict and then find out if ice melts more quickly in a warm place than in a cool place.

Method
Place cubes of ice in different places and see which melt first.

Results
Shade in the boxes until the ice cube has melted.

Place	Time to melt (every box represents __ mins)	Total time

Conclusion
What did you find out?

_____

_____

_____

PHOTOCOPIABLE

CURRICULUM FOCUS • MATERIALS 99

CHAPTER 10

All steamed up

TEACHERS' NOTES

Water to steam

An electric kettle will heat water to 100°C. Most will then cut off automatically as the water begins to boil. If the kettle were to stay on, the water would never rise above 100°C. The extra heat energy would go into turning water to steam and eventually the kettle would boil dry.

Steam, also known as water vapour, is a colourless and clear gas. Since we cannot see it, this explains the comparative lack of awareness of water in this form. The misty cloudy stuff that you do see above a kettle is not steam but water in the form of tiny droplets that are so small they can float about in the air. Clouds are also made up of water droplets – if they were made of steam they, too, would be invisible and we would never have a cloudy day.

So where is the steam? The steam does exist and can be seen in a clear area just above the spout of the kettle. This apparently empty area is very dangerous because the steam is above 100°C and has extra heat reserves that make it burn more strongly than boiling water. As the invisible steam hits the colder air it cools and changes (condenses) into the tiny water droplets that can be seen. Even without kettles, water vapour exists in the air around us. This can be seen by the way in which condensation forms on cold objects placed in a warm room or in the misting of a mirror when we breathe on it. Hygrometers are devices that measure the humidity of the air. Some people have these in their homes or workplaces, although they are not as common as thermometers. Museums often have hygrometers dotted around because the correct humidity is important for preserving the exhibits. Very humid climates exist in places where there are a lot of water and a lot of heat such as in the tropics. Low humidity conditions occur in deserts as one might expect but also in very cold places like Antarctica where any moisture in the air has long ago been frozen out.

Liquid, gas and the water cycle

At sufficiently high temperatures liquids turn to gas – this is called the 'boiling point' (100°C for water). When gases cool down, they turn back to a liquid, again at this same temperature. Even below the boiling point these effects occur but do so more slowly, so that a puddle evaporates even though it is not at boiling point. This change from solid to liquid to gas and back again can occur indefinitely. These changes are essential in the water cycle where water passes through various stages.

- Water in the oceans evaporates to form clouds.
- The clouds drop rain on the ground.
- The rain flows into rivers then back into the oceans.

This cycle repeats itself continuously, the water going through a natural recycling process.

Just as the changes between solid and liquid are described as 'reversible' so too is the change between liquid and gas. As with the change from water to ice, children do not need to use the term 'reversible' but should be aware that the change from water to steam can go both ways.

Safety notes

Steam is potentially more harmful than boiling water and should be treated with great care. The experiment with steam is a demonstration – it is not advisable to let children participate at all in this.
Water should be kept well away from mains electricity.

All steamed up

LESSON PLAN

> **Science objectives (Unit 2D)**
> • To know that water turns to steam when it is heated but on cooling the steam turns back to water.

Resources

- Electric kettle and water
- Small mirror
- Cold container (for example, a chilled drink can wrapped in a towel to keep condensation from forming).

This chapter is a demonstration of changing water to steam (and back) and is a whole-class activity.

Starting points: *whole class*

Set up the demonstration of boiling water and ask the children to gather round, ensuring they maintain a safe distance.

Ask them questions such as:

- What happens to ice when we heat it?
- What happens to water when we heat it?
- When we heat ice it turns into water. What do you think water turns into when we heat it?
- What happens to water when it boils?

Show the children the water being heated in the electric kettle and it boiling. Because of the automatic cut-out the water may boil only for a few seconds so the children must be ready to watch and observe both the cloud of steam and the clear patch just above the spout of the kettle. Some kettles do not have an automatic cut-out though these have become increasingly rare.

Discuss/point out the following.

- There is a clear area where there appears to be nothing.
- Steam is invisible.
- The misty cloud above the kettle is not steam but tiny drops of water.
- The tiny drops of water come from the steam cooling down.
- Clouds, fog and mist are all made from tiny drops of water that float around.
- Steam can be extremely hot, can burn and therefore is dangerous.
- There is a certain amount of invisible water in the air around us.

Demonstrate that this invisible water exists by making some condense on a cold container – it can be held near to the steam rising from the kettle taking appropriate precautions. In a warm room you may find it will mist up from the vapour in the air. Ask for a volunteer to breathe onto a small mirror and explain that the misting up happens because water vapour in your breath cools and turns back to water when it hits the mirror.

Group activities

Activity sheet 1
This sheet is for children who, after having observed the demonstration, can indicate the principles involved by ticking appropriate boxes and recording the result of the experiment by labelling a supplied diagram. The children are also asked to try a simple group experiment (breathing onto a cold metal teaspoon) to test for steam in their breath and to record their results by ticking boxes.

Activity sheet 2
This sheet is for children who, having observed the demonstration, can record the principles by the completion of sentences and produce a record of the results by drawing and labelling a diagram. They are also asked to try a simple group experiment (breathing onto a cold metal teaspoon) to test for steam in their breath and to record their results by completing sentences.

Activity sheet 3
This sheet is aimed at more able children who, having observed the demonstration, can record the results by drawing and labelling a diagram and can record a summary of the experiment given key

words to include. In the subsequent group experiment (breathing onto a cold metal teaspoon), they test for steam in their breath, record their results and then go on to investigate what happens when a warm spoon is used in the experiment.

Plenary session

Discuss the experiment outcomes and anything discovered or that has arisen about:

- water boiling to form steam
- steam being invisible but nevertheless existing in the air
- steam cooling and turning back to water.

Ideas for support

A large chart, as suggested in Chapter 9, could be provided with the words (and possibly pictures depicting) ice, water and steam with arrows labelled 'heat' and 'cool' to indicate what causes the change.

A scene that includes the sun, a puddle and clouds could be used as a visual aid in explaining the principles. A 'water' label should be placed on the puddle, 'steam' labels (several) in the apparently empty air between the sun and the clouds, and 'water droplets' labels on the clouds themselves.

Ideas for extension

The children could try an evaporation experiment where they put small dishes of water in different locations and see how long it is before the water evaporates/turns to steam.

Linked ICT activities

Using a graphics program, such as 'Granada Colours', 'Fresco' or 'Dazzle', show the children how to use the paintbrush and fill tools. Tell them that they are only going to use the colour white to draw a picture like the one they drew on the steamed up mirror. Set the page up by filling the page with black colour. Show the children how to change the colour to white or grey and how to use the paintbrush and fill tools to create their picture. Show them how to save the picture and how to change the colour of the background by filling the background a different colour. Ask the children to choose which background colour they think looks the best colour.

Name _____

All steamed up

ACTIVITY SHEET 1

Your teacher will show you how water can be turned into steam and how to turn steam back to water.

Label this picture of a boiling kettle to show:

water   steam   a cloud of tiny drops of water

Tick the correct boxes.

Water is turned to steam by	cooling it ☐	heating it ☐
Steam is turned to water by	cooling it ☐	heating it ☐

Breathing experiment
Breathe on a cold metal teaspoon about ten times. Look at the spoon carefully.

Is there some water on the spoon?	yes ☐	no ☐
Is there steam in my breath?	yes ☐	no ☐

PHOTOCOPIABLE

CURRICULUM FOCUS • MATERIALS 103

Name _____

All steamed up

ACTIVITY SHEET 2

Your teacher will show you how water can be turned into steam and how to turn steam back to water.

Draw a picture of a boiling kettle. Put labels on the picture to show:

water steam a cloud of tiny drops of water

Complete the following sentences:

Water is turned to steam by _____

Steam is turned to water by _____

Breathing experiment

Breathe on a cold metal teaspoon about ten times. Look at the spoon carefully.

After breathing on the spoon I see _____

This means that there is _____ in the air we breathe out.

104 CURRICULUM FOCUS • MATERIALS

PHOTOCOPIABLE

Name _____

All steamed up

ACTIVITY SHEET 3

Your teacher will show you how water can be turned into steam and how to turn steam back to water.

Draw a picture of a boiling kettle. Put labels on the picture to show:

water   steam   a cloud of tiny drops of water

```
┌─────────────────────────────────────┐
│                                     │
│                                     │
│                                     │
│                                     │
│                                     │
│                                     │
│                                     │
└─────────────────────────────────────┘
```

On the back of this sheet, write a sentence about how to change water to steam. Write another sentence about how to change steam back to water. Your sentences should include the words: cooling   heating

Breathing experiment

Breathe on a cold metal teaspoon about ten times. Look at the spoon carefully.

What do you notice?

Is there steam in the air we breathe out?

Try this with a warm spoon. Try to explain the difference.

Extra!

Design a different experiment to find the warmest place in the classroom. Hint – perhaps you could use small dishes of water.

PHOTOCOPIABLE

CURRICULUM FOCUS • MATERIALS   105

Useful resources

Resources recommended for linked ICT activities

Software

Counter for Windows, Granada Learning/ Blackcat Software, Granada Television, Quay Street, Manchester M60 9EA, Tel 0161 827 2927 www.granada-learning.com

My World, Granada Learning/SEMERC, Granada Television, Quay Street, Manchester M60 9EA, Tel 0161 827 2927 www.granada-learning.com

Textease 2000, Softease and Textease 2000 (PC), Softease Ltd, Market Place, Ashbourne, Derbyshire DE6 1ES, Tel 01335 343 421, Fax 01335 343 422; www.softease.com

Talking Write Away, Granada Learning/ Blackcat Software, Granada Television, Quay Street, Manchester M60 9EA, Tel 0161 827 2927, www.granada-learning.com

Dazzle, Fresco Granada Learning, Granada Television, Quay Street, Manchester M60 9EA, Tel 0161 827 2927, www.granada-learning.com

Pick a picture, **Granada Colours,** Granada Learning, Granada Television, Quay Street, Manchester M60 9EA, Tel 0161 827 2927, www.granada-learning.com

Valiant Roamer, Valiant Technology, [address] www.valiant-technology.com/ideas1.htm

Clicker 4, Crick Software Ltd, Tel:-01604 671691 www.cricksoft.com

Digital camera
Digital Dream 'L'Elegante' digital camera for children: TAG Learning, Tel 01474 357 350, Fax 01474 537 887; www.taglearning.co.uk